THE FUTURE BELONGS TO THOSE WHO ARE

FAST

Cheers !

The Best of the Insight from JimCarroll.com

by

Jim Carroll

OBLIO Press, www.obliopress.com

Carroll, Jim, 1959-
    The Future Belongs to Those Who are Fast / Jim Carroll.

ISBN 978-0-9736554-4-5

Production Credits:
Editors: Christa Carroll
Cover Design: Laurence Smink
Photography: R. Kelly Clipperton

Printed in Canada

Table of Contents

To Christa
For reminding me that even though the future might belong to those who are fast, there are times when it's ok to slow things down.

To Willie and Thomas
For being such wonderful young men!

Introduction

I have a pretty unique job. I spend a lot of my time challenging people to think about innovation and the future, whether it is for a conference of 1000's or a small CEO/Board meeting of 10-15 people.

In preparing for these events, I have the opportunity to talk to a lot of different people about the trends impacting their organizations. I also do an extensive amount of research that helps me to understand the future that they face.

What I have learned over time, regardless of the industry or group, is that the pace of change that we have seen in the last few years is not going to slow down - the future does truly belong to those who are fast.

The future doesn't belong to those who have owned a market place because of their history. Past success doesn't guarantee a future of winning. Resting on ones laurels is perhaps the best method to place yourself at the greatest risk in the future.

We live in a world in which business models evolve at a furious pace. In which customers are demanding and expecting new forms of interaction. In which technology and mobile devices are changing industries at a furious pace. Everywhere you look, you witness rates of change and innovation which are accelerating, not slowing down.

That leads to an undeniable fact - it will be the ability of an individual, a leader, and an organization to keep up with fast paced change that will increasingly define their potential for future success.

But for many people, it is often difficult to find the time to discover the trends that might impact them, or think about the issues of innovation that they should be thinking about.

Back in 2002 when blogs became part of the online world, I decided to start documenting some of my observations on trends, innovation and creative thinking from my various keynotes onto my own blog, which I maintain at JimCarroll.com. At this point, there are almost a thousand entries, but there are a few that seem to resonate with people more than others, hence this book.

I have taken what I think are some of the most popular, relevant and useful observations from the blog and combined them into this book, The Future Belongs to Those Who Are Fast. My intent was to provide an easy way to discover some of what I have learned through what has become a truly remarkable job.

Enjoy!

Jim

How to Battle
Organizational Sclerosis!

A few years ago, when I was the closing speaker for the Swiss Innovation Forum in Zurich, I made the observation that many organizations fail because they have failure engrained in their corporate culture!

Do you?

It can be difficult to try to be innovative in many organizations. People with an innovation-oriented mindset often find their enthusiasm stymied when they approach senior management with an initiative. And when their effort is turned back, it can be extremely frustrating!

One of the most typical situations today in which we are seeing innovation-dead-in-its-tracks involves the many initiatives that people are pursuing with social networks and/or mobile applications. They know that we live in transformative times in which major changes are occurring with branding, production, promotion, customer relationships and just about everything else!

So they set off to build a sophisticated customer-oriented Facebook initiative; they roll out a prototype mobile iPhone app; or they simply get a very basic Twitter feed happening that includes a stream of useful news updates that customers might actually appreciate.

Enthusiastic as heck, they take their project to the senior management team — and it's rejected, with a litany of reasons as to why the organization just isn't ready to deal with their new ideas right now. Any number of reasons can be given; each and every one of them is indicative of the fact that a sort of organizational sclerosis has set in, that clogs up the ability of the organization to deal with anything new.

Consider the attitudes that you might encounter if you are trying to get something happening:

- we don't understand it, so we don't think we need to do it

- it's too easy to not confront the tough issues

- we are too busy fighting fires right now

- we don't have the skill sets to deal with this

- we haven't thought about this in our strategic planning process

- we haven't really spent a lot of time thinking about what comes next

- we don't have a budget for that

- what we've been doing all along is perfectly ok, isn't it?

- there's so much going on, and we don't know where it might fit in terms of priorities

- it's too far ahead of its time.

Of course, it's easy to take this wall of negativity, step back from the project, curb your enthusiasm — and give up!

But real innovators don't give up! They work to address the organizational sclerosis that might be in place. What you should do is confront these excuses head on. There are a variety of different reactions depending on the different excuses that are used:

- **If they don't understand it, educate them!** This might involve building a better business case for the initiative, bringing them up to date on the key business drivers and trends that require some bold steps and dramatic change.

- **Help them to realize that those who tackle the tough issues usually win.** This is a good time to put into perspective the concept of accelerating change. You need to make sure that the leadership team understands that everything around us today is changing faster than ever before, and will continue to do so: business models; methods of customer interaction; new forms of competition. Business today is all about continually confronting a flood of tough issues. We should be bulking up our capabilities to deal with a world of incessant change.

- **If the organization is always in fire-fighting mode, change the agenda.** Maybe they won't be fighting as many fires over the long term if they have a clear view of the future and have a strategy that aligns to that future. So rather than asking, "whoah, where'd that come from," they're asking "ok, what comes next, and what do we need to do about it?"

- **Get the skill sets that you need.** If there are shortfalls in certain key skills to deal with current business realities, deal with it and fix it fast. Ensure that you work with HR to undertake a skills inventory with respect to the area you are trying to innovate within, and work to plug the holes.

- **If it's not part of the strategic planning process, make it part of it.** Every organization has multiple processes in which issues and activities rise to the top because they've been identified as fitting within the overall strategic plan. If yours isn't part of the plan, work to get it there; and again, this comes through education, a clear business case, as well as internal discussions with those who are involved with and shape the strategic planning process.

- **Get people thinking about what comes next.** Does the organization have a regular series of forward looking leadership meetings? Does it take the time to assess the trends which might impact it on a 1, 2, 5 and 10 year basis? Is it busy looking at "have we really spent a lot of time thinking about what comes next."

- **We don't have a budget for that!** Following the process of getting the initiative into the strategic plan will help to lead to the next step: getting the project properly approved and funded within the overall budget process for the organization. There's a process for budgeting. You have to be intimately involved in and respect the process.

- **Make it clear that it isn't ok to keep doing the same thing that has been done in the past.** You've got to clearly articulate the new threats the organization faces and the opportunities that it can pursue as a result of ongoing change.

- **In the high velocity economy, it is extremely easy for people to feel absolutely overwhelmed in terms of placing priorities.** With so much change happening, it is difficult to know exactly what to do, where to start, how to focus, and to not obsess over doing the wrong thing. The easiest reaction when faced with such feelings is to simply pull back and do nothing. That's the absolutely worse thing you can be doing. Take on some projects to keep your innovation capabilities fresh and up to date, and to give you better insight into what issues might be priorities and which ones are not.

- **It's too far ahead of its time.** This type of thinking might have made sense in the 20th century when the world, market, industries, products and customers changed at a slow and steady and predictable pace. That type of thinking has been thrown out on its ear - what might seem far-fetched right now is likely to be very real tomorrow, and maybe even out of date and replaced with something else by the time you get to it!

In Zurich, I noted that we develop corporate cultures that stifle our ability to try to do anything new. That's what you've got to work to avoid — it's not easy to do — but absolutely necessary!

What Do World Class Innovators Do That Others Don't Do?

One of my keynote events was for the leadership team of a company that's involved in a sector of the construction industry. They've had some challenges with the economic downturn, they're also likely to see a resurgence as infrastructure spending kicks in. But they're thinking beyond what happens after that — they're positioning themselves for long term growth — and so they brought me in to stir up some creative thinking as to what they need to do.

The focus of my keynote was: "What is it that world class innovators do that other organizations don't do?" Here's some of the insight that I covered.

World class innovators possess a relentless focus on growth

I deal with a lot of CEO's at a lot of organizations, and in almost every instance, they've engaged me because my message of future growth opportunities resonates with their own attitude. In my view, there are unprecedented opportunities for growth in almost every industry. We live in transformative times that offer tremendous opportunities for growth through innovation.

World class innovators continually transition their revenue source

They're focused on 'chameleon revenue.' They know that they have to evolve from being a commodity product competing on price, to one that offers a more complex, revenue rich solution. They're aware that they need to have continuous, relentless product innovation in order to keep their new revenue pipeline full.

World class innovators solve customers problems before the customer knows it's a problem

They excel at anticipatory thinking: where do we need to go with our customers to ensure that we continue to have a strong revenue relationship? What key trends can we ride to maximum advantage that will allow us to provide a constant flood of new, irresistible innovations for our customer base?

World class innovators source innovation ideas through their customers

Simply put, they derive new innovation ideas by observing what their customers are doing with their products or services. They know that they aren't fully in control of the innovation agenda anymore, and that some of the most brilliant ideas are coming from a new source. One VP put it this way:

> We have the advantage of working with some of the most innovative people in the world. For example, we could find a customer who is using one of our products in an unexpected and innovative way. It's then possible for us to take that and add value for another customer, which is one of the ways we can help the innovation process as a whole.
> *John Hanks, vice-president, Industrial and Embedded Products for National Instruments, www.theengineer.co.uk*

World class innovators focus on ingesting fast ideas

There are new technologies, business models, customer trends, product developments, scientific advances and countless other things that are increasing the pace of change. Innovators know that if they plug into the global idea machine, they can constantly discover a tremendous number of insights that help them to move forward.

World class innovators check their speed and focus on corporate agility

They know they need to keep up with the fast paced trends. Their future success lies in their ability to quickly act and react. There's not a lot of time for debate or study; inertia is abhorred. They simply DO.

World class innovators focus on long term wins through constant incremental improvements

They know that some pretty big growth can come from continual small wins and improvement on margins. For example, 7% of power on transmission and distribution lines are lost as heat. Reduce that loss by 10% and that would equal all the new wind power installed in the U.S. in 2006. That's why 'smart grids' are such a hot topic. Another example is the auto industry: today's typical automotive system uses only 25% of the energy in the tank — the balance is lost to waste, heat, inefficiency. Work on increasing that on a year over year basis, and there are some pretty solid gains through innovation.

World class innovators focus on skills partnerships as a key success factor

They know that with rapid change, knowledge is becoming an ever more precious commodity, particularly niche oriented knowledge. If they are entering a fascinating new, fast paced market, they realize that there might be but a few individuals or organizations in the world who could help them tackle that new market. They focus on forming fast teams and fast partnerships, drawing a lot of innovation oxygen from that external insight.

World class innovators focus on pervasive connectivity for next generation products

They know that one of the key trends over the next ten years or so is that everything around us will plug together. Soon, every device on the planet will have an IP address on the Internet, we'll be able to access its status and its location. This is transformative stuff, and is one of the primary sources for the next new billions of dollars of revenue in countless industries. Consider the world of HVAC (industrial heating, ventilation and air conditioning) equipment as it is transitioned to the world of HVAC 2.0, an intelligent, interlinked, fascinating new world of massive connectivity.

World class innovators aren't afraid to back great ideas

They know that right now is a great time to made bold decisions, and take decisive advantage to forge aggressive new paths against their competitors. While everyone else wallows in aggressive indecision and organizational sclerosis, world class innovators know that it is a great time to do great things.

*   *   *   *   *

You know what? World class innovators win!

A newspaper headline from some time in the future

Ten Fundamental Trends That Don't Change with the Meltdown

I wrote this blog post a few weeks after the global economic crisis of 2008 began. It provides useful guidance any time there is economic uncertainty in the future.

You and I know that the headline above is going to run in newspapers and mainstream media one day. The BIG question is when.

So what are the trends that will drive future growth? Off the top of my head, there are several:

- **Growth markets will continue to emerge.** Back in the 19th century, the head of the U.S. Patent Office stated that *"everything that can be invented has been invented."* Such silliness. Right now, there are hundreds of thousands of new products, markets, industries and ideas being built and explored. The future isn't over. Its arrival has just slowed a degree.

- **Leaders in existing markets will grow through innovation.** My own gut feel is that there are a lot of organizations out there approaching this recession differently. They're innovating in their markets; they're working on customer retention; they're investing in customer service in order to keep competitive; they're talking about how to grow in a down market. People want to talk about innovation and the future. That's a great sign that the recovery is underway.

- **Health care will see significant transformation, not to mention spending.** Health care is transitioning to a system of predictive medicine. This is a huge, long term, 20 year trend, that has big implications with the emergence of new careers, industries, professions, and companies. DNA based medicine is a massive change. On top of that, the mere level of spending that is going to occur in managing the looming health care crisis will drive all kinds of growth, though the funding part of the equation will remain a big problem. The result? Lots of innovative thinking on how to solve huge problems with unique solutions.

- **'Green' and 'energy' will continue to have momentum.** Some argue that the meltdown will defer everything having to do with these two efforts. I disagree. I think the corporate sector has discovered the cost benefit that comes from green projects, and so they will continue to invest, which will drive innovation. Globally, I think we've passed the point where people and their leaders believe that doing the same old thing as in the past is going to continue in the future. I don't see leading edge research into solar, wind, and other alternatives slowing down any time soon. The fascinating thing is that there is a lot of backyard, garage tinkering going on right now, and that's where the next product/market breakthroughs will come from.

- **Technology will continue to hyper-innovate.** I've got six generations of Blackberry's that span about six years or less. Likewise, iPhone's have become the coolest fashion statement on the planet for the younger demographic. The Internet-enabled thermostat I have in my home and chalet is the first step in a huge wave of pervasive connectivity. I don't see hi-tech innovation and R&D slowing down. Indeed, during the last recession, some of the biggest innovations — the iPod, the iPad — emerged from the minds of those inventing the future. There are a lot more billion-dollar markets still to emerge.

- **Agility and flexibility will dominate.** In the next several years, the manufacturing industry — globally and locally — will learn to do what Honda has done: focus on rapid assembly and reassembly capabilities, making them able to quickly change models and products to respond to fast paced consumer demand. As they do so, they'll undergo a fundamental transformation in their thinking, structure and capabilities that will ensure their success.

- **The global idea machine will continue to influence innovation.** The Internet continues to have a profound impact on everything we do. Scientific discovery is speeding up. New discoveries continue to go forward at a furious pace. Eco-building design concepts are debated, shared and then go global in an instant. From the global mind comes unprecedented innovation, new products, new companies and new industries.

- **The next generation takes over.** The boomers are a dispirited bunch right now; there's not a lot of passion and enthusiasm with some of them to change the future, particularly given the status of their 401K's. Some in the younger generation are witnessing their first ever generation, and it's probably pretty terrifying. (This is my 4th, so I'm an old hand at this.) Yet, they're a hardy, entrepreneurial bunch, who have grown up with a mindset that inhales change, pursues multiple different opportunities, and collaborates like nothing we've ever seen before. I think they'll shake things up pretty quickly.

- **A faster world happens, well, faster.** Simply put, faster news cycles means that people get through difficult periods faster, at least in terms of mindset. Do you think people are moving to the acceptance phase quicker? I believe they are, and I think this faster attitude shift, compared to a slower pace of acceptance in previous recessions, means that innovation will drive us out of this faster than we expect.

- **Transformative thinking drives growth.** Last but not least, we can't discount the impact of a new American mindset upon the global economy. It seems clear that a decisive mandate has been delivered by the American populace that they want to rejoin the global economy, and want to work hard and fast to fix the problems that have resulted. Big change comes from big ideas sponsored by leaders with big dreams.

I dunno, I'm hugely optimistic. How about you?

The Case for Optimism & Global Economic Recovery

One of my recent events was to speak at the annual meeting of a financial group. The audience included a large cross section of business executives from throughout the Midwest of America. My talk centered around the trends that might provide for sustainable economic growth. Here's what I focused on:

- **A significant and lasting change in perspective.** I spend a lot of time with major international organizations, either in strategic leadership meetings or at various association events or conferences. I often run a text message poll at the start of such sessions to gauge the audience perspective of the current rate of economic growth. I've seen quite a change in attitude and perspective in the last few months.

- **Significant growth is emerging from "solving the big problems."** I am a big believer that the efforts to solve the big challenges with respect to energy, the environment and health care will provide the momentum to kickstart the economy once again. I spend a lot of time examining signs of innovation and growth, and there is a tremendous amount of mind share being devoted to each of these areas.

- **Fundamental and long lasting growth trends in global markets.** Before the economy went sour in 2008, McKinsey was extremely bullish on the prospects for economic growth driven by the rapid industrialization of emerging economies, noting that "*almost a billion new consumers will enter the global marketplace in the next decade .... with an income level that allows spending on discretionary goods,*" and that "*the ranks of the middle class will swell by 1.8 billion to become 52% of total population, up from 30% today.*" I think on a long term basis, those trends are still valid and will provide for tremendous economic growth.

- **A rapid response of organizations to the fast emergence of new markets and opportunities.** I am seeing a significant number of organizations whose top level is focused on "revenue innovation," that is, generating revenue by entering new markets or through new products and solutions. One CEO of a major global organization put it to me this way: "*traditional markets are declining ... we're going other places that have better growth opportunities.*" This is the concept of chameleon revenue.

- **Signs of various industries reinventing themselves.** China, India and Brazil are cleaning our clocks when it comes to manufacturing, with sheer brainpower and design capabilities. The period from 1990 to 2010 saw the decline of the North American manufacturing industry with resultant massive economic shock. But what I'm seeing out there tells me that North American companies will learn to compete again by challenging old assumptions, and by challenging themselves to do things differently this time around with mass customization, and through the reinvention of traditional manufacturing processes.

- **The emergence of intelligent infrastructure.** Quite simply, every device around us is going to gain intelligence in the next decade. We'll have awareness of their status, location, and IP address; this leads to the birth of countless new products, companies and industries. Real transformative industry growth will come when everything plugs into the cloud, and location intelligence becomes a significant transformative trend.

- **The impact of the next generation.** While many people bemoan the 'work ethic' of Gen-Y, I think they are likely the most entrepreneurial generation ever. They collaborate, think, and generate ideas in exciting and different ways, and I think that provides them with the motivation to "do their own thing" unlike any other generation in history. That is a significant driver for economic growth. During the recession of 2001, 569,750 new companies were created in North America – mostly small businesses. Companies with less than 20 employees accounted for 100% of the new job growth from 1990 to 2000. Global experience shows similar trends. That's the context of what this 'next generation' will do.

As a futurist, I'm optimistic and bullish on the future. (I have to be; I can't quite go on stage and say to people — "guess what — your future sucks!"). I don't think there is any wishful thinking behind this sentiment, it comes from the discussions and observations I get from going out and speaking to tens of thousands of people at various conferences and events.

I continaully challenge my personal sentiments about the future in order to stay focused on opportunity. Don't you think that might be a good frame of mind that you should adopt as well? After all, some people see the future and see a threat — innovators see the same future, and see nothing but opporunity. Often, by concious choice.

Transformative Trends
Major Issues That You Need to Start Thinking About Now!

How small is your world? Are you thinking BIG enough in terms of just how many big trends are going to impact your future?

Many people ask me how I nail down many of the trends that will redefine society, industries, markets and nations into the future. It involves a lot of research and a great deal of listening to other experts. But it also comes from the fact that I spend my time as a speaker at corporate meetings, massive association events and board retreats, with the resultant opportunity of seeing what many of the most innovative organizations in the world are focused on. Just take a look at my client list, and you'll get a sense that I have a constant stream of global executive level insight that drives my view of the future.

My trending observations also involves a lot of common sense. Take the "expectation gap" which I outline below. This is a pretty significant trend, and it's pretty well blindingly obvious when you think about it.

So what comes next? Here's a quick list of 10 trends that you could be thinking about that provide for significant transformative change. Let's continue to innovate our way into the future!

The Expectation Gap

It's one of the most obvious, most significant, and most challenging trends going forward into the future. Quite simply, Western society is defined by an increasing divergence between what people expect, and what they will get.

- People expect the world's greatest health care services but with the aging of society, it is dramatically clear that the system won't be able to deliver what they expect.

- Boomers expect that they will have comfortable retirement pensions; the economic reset and collapsing home values have made it increasingly clear that their hopes will likely have been dashed.

- People expect that they can live longer, but the increasing prevalence of lifestyle diseases due to obesity and other factors means that in some areas of the Western world, 60 is the new 70.

- People expect that they can reduce the size of "big government" but have no sense of just how to go about doing this without a great deal of pain.

Whatever the case may be, our future is increasingly defined by this gap, and it is going to have huge ramifications for just about everything around us. The reality: a lot of organizations are going to make a lot of money in helping to close the gap! Take health care and what is really going to happen in terms of future trends. Huge opportunities for growth!

Industries Blur

In the past, we've had "industries" which have focused on particular products and markets. Increasingly, the concept of an "industry" is going to blur as fascinating new trends provide interesting new opportunities.

Consider this: the world of fashion and healthcare are going to merge. We are going to see an increasing number of bio-connectivity health care devices that will be used for the remote monitoring of health care conditions. Quite simply, people will increasingly wear small "smart appliances" that will monitor their compliance with exercise programs or that will keep their doctors up to date with key health indicators.

But people won't want to wear medical appliances: they'll want to wear fashion! Health-care jewelry anyone?

Energy Gets Smart

Clearly we're going to see continued high-speed innovation with renewable energy sources, and velocity with grid-parity: the point in time at which the cost of producing renewable energy equals that of carbon based sources. Much of this is coming about as Silicon Valley gets aggressively involved in the energy sector. Taiwan Semiconductor, one of the largest chip manufacturers in the world, has invested $193 million in solar-cell maker Motech Industries.

That's but a small example of a major trend in which hi-tech companies are getting aggressively involved in every single aspect of the renewable energy marketplace. Just look at what Google is up to with wind-farms off the Eastern Seaboard!

The Collapse of Attention Spans

Everything changes when people lose their ability to focus: sports, shopping, living.....the numbers with the next generation of consumers are simply staggering. The average teen sent 435 text messages per month in 2007; it's now 2899! That's 97 messages per day, an increase of 566% in just a few years.

It's estimated that they now spend 7.5 hours a day engaged with some type of media screen; if you add in the fact they are multitasking, it comes out to 11 hours of screen time per day — or 53 hours a week. That's more time than most are involved in a full time job!

What's the impact? Continued hyper-speed in the evolution of branding and advertising; surreal rates of change involving products and services; unbelievable rates of change in how decisions are made and people are influenced. If you don't know how to think, market and promote at nano-speeds, you're not ready for the future!

Faster Market Evolution

If we're thinking faster, than we are innovating faster! New products flood the market at ever increasing speeds, and fast-consumers snap them up in a moment and evolve their lifestyles quicker. We're all going to begin moving at Apple-speed as Silicon Valley increasingly comes to control the pace of innovation in many industries. Put it this way: it took two years for Apple to sell two million iPhones, but only 2 months for them to sell 2 million iPads! And just about a month to sell 1 million iPhone 4's!

We're seeing the same trend in many other industries and product lines: the business of outsourcing the manufacturing LCD TV's exploded from $9.4 billion in 2009 to over $21 billion in 2010, and an estimated $30 billion in 2011. Some products are obsolete before they are released: Lenovo learned this fact when they cancelled their planned "tablet computer" due to the unbelievably fast success of the Apple iPad.

Innovation Partnerships

Given this rate of change, companies are quickly learning that in this fast paced world, they can't innovate on their own, it is simply too difficult to keep up. They've realized that they can enjoy greater success through open innovation and other external innovation partnerships.

A great example of what happens when innovation "opens up" is seen with the partnership between consumer appliance maker Phillips and Sarah Lee on the single-serving coffee machines. It's a market that grew from nothing to 12 million machines and 7 billion coffee "pods" in just 5 short years!

Everywhere I go, I see organizations focused on challenging the core concepts of how they do "new things." There's a new mindset, and this is going to drive a big part of the growth for organizations going into the future.

The Fight Against Workplace Boredom

When there's so much fun and fast change in the world, a job can be a mind-numbing experience. That's why one survey suggested that 67% of Gen-Y admitted that on their very first day on a new job they were already thinking about another job.

Organizations are fighting back against boredom by trying to keep staff engaged. At IBM's Bromont Canada plant, the "3×10" program aims to combat workplace boredom by changing employees full set of responsibilities 3 times every 10 years. The program is managed by someone who has worked in 10 different jobs within the plant over the last 28 years. Expect within a few years the likelihood that a "3×10" program will have shifted to a "2×1" program.

American-Idolatry

People love competition, they love winners, and they relish the battle! Everyone is learning that if they are to succeed in the future, they have to appeal to the new base of hero-worship that comes from our new awards driven society. Everywhere I go, I see companies who are far more willing to celebrate and elevate heroes. DHL holds an annual innovation day which includes an award ceremony with partners who have worked with them on innovative ideas. Deloitte South Africa hosts an annual "Best Company To Work For" survey and combines into it an elaborate awards ceremony. The future of workplace and partner renumeration is all about the red-carpet, the spotlight, and the celebration of success!

The Big Impact of Small Incrementalism

Everyone is learning that one way to win in the future is by having a lot of small wins that add up to big gains:

- The oil industry currently retrieves only 1 out of 3 barrels per well on average, yet a 1% improvement represents huge revenue gains!

- 7% of power on transmission and distribution lines is lost as heat, yet reduce that loss by 10% and that would equal all the new wind power installed in the U.S. in 2006.

- Today's typical automotive system uses only 25% of the energy in the tank — the balance is lost to waste, heat, inefficiency. Work on increasing that on a year over year basis, and there are some pretty solid gains through innovation.

- At DuPont, the savings are adding up: globally they now produce 40% more material using the same amount of energy they used in 1990.

- Up to 30% of the energy used in a typical industrial or commercial building today is wasted, but new, incremental improvements in green building design and other eco-principles are fixing this fast.

Every industry I am dealing with sees small marginal wins adding up to huge tactical advantages! Small is the new winner.

Communities Redefined

There were 37 million senior citizens in the U.S. in 2006, or about 12% of the population. By 2030, there will be 71.5 million of them, representing 20% of the population. Other nations in the Western world are seeing the same trend: we're all about to become like Japan! The reality of funding issues means it will be impossible to have the same seniors-housing or assisted living type of infrastructure that we've had in the past. The next generation of retirees are going to live at home longer; they'll live with each other more; the hippies of the 60's are going to find themselves in the seniors communes of 2015! Community-bliss: far out, man!

What does it mean? Communities are going to have to be rethought, redesigned and reconstructed – community ergonomics is going to be a massive growth industry! Overall, we'll see a lot more growth in high density, compact, mixed-use communities – and a lot of innovative thinking as to what the concept of 'community' means.

*   *   *   *   *

Think about these trends from this perspective — there is a lot of transformative change that is underway. This is no time to think "small." This is the time you need to be thinking "big." How "small" is your world: do you have a narrow view of opportunity? The reality is that right now, thinking BIG in terms of opportunity and the future will be crucial to your future success.

What does that mean for your future? In the old days, companies had "industries" that they worked within, "markets" that they sold into, and "business models" that they pursued. Assumptions that drove their decisions. Every single assumption that you might have about your future could be wrong. Challenge those assumptions, think about the rapidity of future trends, innovate — and you'll find the growth opportunities that seem to elude so many others.

Innovation
and the Concept of
Chameleon Revenue

One of the most significant things you need to think about is how you are going to continually reinvent your business to keep up with fast-paced change.

In many cases this will involve structural change based on an acceleration of business cycles. Consider manufacturing, for example. We're moving from a world of mass production to mass customization, or what I call agility-based manufacturing. I often cite the case of Honda, as noted in an article on the financial website Bloomberg: "*Honda's assembly lines can switch models in as little as 10 days.*" By contrast, the article suggests, it could take months for most rivals to make the same change.

Companies such as Honda can see what's selling strongly and quickly reorient their production to fit that demand. In the meantime, its competitors are busy cranking out 700,000 versions of the same old car, hoping to sell it to consumers who have already moved on to something different. It's no wonder Detroit is being killed off by its long-term reliance on gas-guzzlers.

Everyone now understands that the old Detroit-based manufacturing business model was deeply flawed. The newer model, based on agility and flexibility, is the model of the future. If an organization can rapidly change its production to accommodate what consumers are willing to buy, it has a good chance of future success.

This ability to respond quickly to change is the corner-stone of opportunity. Competitors will emerge, particularly as the new connected generation rejects existing business models and innovative people continue to shake up the fundamentals. Take the business model of Wizzit, a South African cellphone-based banking system, which could cause upheaval throughout the banking sector as mobile technology garners more of our attention.

Furthermore, the nano-cannibalization of markets is becoming a business trend rather than an aberration. For example, Apple broke new ground years ago by tossing out an entire iPod Nano product line worth billions of dollars of revenue, replacing it with a newer, up-to-date product. Imagine even considering that. How could it cannibalize its own product revenue?

I recently spoke at a leadership meeting for a global organization, where the CEO spoke of a future in which the company's success would come from what he called "chameleon revenue" – the sales derived from entirely new product lines. The chart he presented said it all: the organization's future consisted of a steady decrease in baseline revenue and accelerating revenue streams from markets it currently does not participate in.

I think this will become the norm for most organizations. The ability to rapidly enter and exit markets will define future success. The ability to sustain multiple, short-term product life cycles, each perhaps no more than 36 to 48 months long, will be a critical success factor. Agility at discovering, producing and capitalizing on new revenue sources will be a fundamental necessity. In other words, your ability to change your spots and your colour on a dime will be the key driver for your potential.

Which begs the question: does your financial system have the capability to provide information on your chameleon revenue streams? Does it provide the insight and analytical tools to tackle product life-cycle revenue so the organization can assess how quickly its chameleon revenue streams are evolving? If it doesn't, what do you need to do to adapt?

Innovation in the Global Energy Industry

The CEO and senior management team of a large global energy company engaged me to provide them with insight on the trends which will impact the global oil, natural gas, energy and distribution sectors in the years to come.

It was a small, intimate get-together with about 40 senior executives. I provided my insight into the trends that I believe will have the most impact. That was followed by about an hour of very intense, deep probing discussion. I believe I stirred up some creative thinking within the group.

These were some of the issues I suggested they start thinking about:

- **Presume massive market disruption.** Think GoogleCar: don't limit your view of the future to what might transpire. The future of any industry will likely bear no resemblance to the industry structure of today. Future competitors will probably come from completely outside of an existing industry. Challenge every assumption that you have about the future.

- **Prepare for significant transformation.** Realize that existing insurmountable challenges are simply a big opportunity to someone else. Someone, somewhere, is going to figure out how to plug hundreds of thousands, if not millions of small, local, home based renewable energy sources into the energy grid. It's mostly a computation/mathematical issue. The energy grid was not designed for two way electricity transmission, and so there will have to be an intense amount of computational dynamics to structure a solution. Result? An organization that is a master of massive computational capabilities — and hence, grid management — might very well be the new energy company of the future.

- **Find opportunity in scientific rapidity.** We're in the era of global collaborative knowledge generation, and R&D is rapidly externalizing. The infinite global idea loop means that scientific discovery is now happening faster than ever before, which provides for more product and market opportunity. Innovative organizations plug in, ensuring that all staff are in tune with the rapid rate of scientific advance that surrounds them, and are prepared to ride new emerging ideas as soon as they begin to emerge.

- **Capitalize on skills fragmentation.** The war for talent will define future success. We're entering a time of massive skills specialization and ever smaller knowledge niches. It's the organizations that can build a culture, structure and flexibility to attract and retain skills that will find the key to success in the high velocity economy.

- **Structure for volatility.** Extreme volatility is the 'new normal.' If you have the capability to quickly adjust strategy, structure, plans, skills, projects and teams, you've got the right stuff for the new world of constant change.

- **Prepare for business intensity.** Innovative organizations plan for more rapid entrance and exits from new markets. They do so through flexible structure. Partnerships take on new roles in an era of exponentiating, fast complexity and the rapid emergence of new opportunities. If you can scale up, you can win big.

The Economist Intelligence Unit recently noted that *"the ability to swiftly adapt to change represents the greatest challenge manufacturers face in creating long-term value."* That's the bottom line for innovating in the high velocity energy industry.

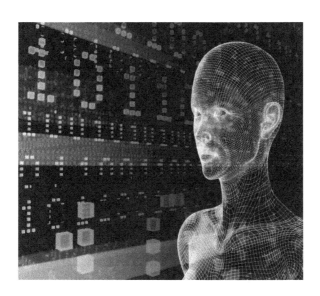

Five More Trends
to Define Your Future

For a few years, I've been observing that "infrastructure is the new plastic." The key theme is that in the future, a global, smart intelligent infrastructure is emerging that will impact transportation, health care, energy and other industries. (The phrase is a play on the theme in the 1960's movie, *The Graduate*, when the kid's dad's friend mentioned "plastics" as being the industry of the future.)

Using that analogy, I spoke in one keynote about large-scale new trends that would provide for substantial growth markets.

- **Analytics.** The future is owned by the math geeks. We're entering an era in which extremely intelligent people who know a lot about how to throw a bunch of computers at a complex problem in order to come up with interesting solutions. Here's an example: backyard energy. Lots of people would like to do their part in helping the environment by having their own back yard solar or wind power station. The problem is that most of the North American electric grid wasn't designed for two way transmission — meaning that you can't pump your excess energy back into the grid. Yet, some smart math dude will come along and come up with a fascinating new load-balancing technology, based on sophisticated mathematics and massive amounts of computer processing power, to solve the problem. There are going to be a lot of unique solutions, and hence, unique industries that are set to unfold.

- **Location-intelligence.** Think about the transformative change that can occur when you link the type of information found in GoogleMaps to existing corporate data. In the insurance industry, individuals are looking at how they can link existing insurance policy information to spatial (i.e. geographic) oriented information, in order to come up with new forms of assessing, understanding and underwriting insurance risk.

- **Pervasive connectivity.** Everything around you is about to become "plugged-in," and life is about to get really strange. One day you'll get up, and your weigh scale will send an e-mail to your fridge. Just kidding, but consider this reality: many of the things that we use in an industrial, commercial or residential setting are about to undergo three distinct transitions. They are gaining intelligence; they will send information that advises us as to their location; and they will update us on their status. Think about what happens when you bring home a box of popcorn, and it interacts with your microwave, linking into a centralized database to determine the best cooking duration for your particular microwave brand.

- **Hyper-innovation.** China is rapidly transitioning from the "made" phase to the "created" stage. Think "Designed in China" as the next big wave that will lead to rapid product innovation. Half the population in China is under the age of 25. They're collaborative, highly educated, and eager to continue the transition into the wealth that comes with being a member of the Chinese middle class. They're about to innovate like crazy, and will soon be flooding our stores with all kinds of innovative consumer products, not to mention stuff for the industrial, health care, packaging and just about every other industry out there. Someone is going to import, support, sell and install this stuff.

- **Skills specialization.** The future of every career is either extremely specialized, or massively general. Most professions are fragmenting into dozens, if not hundreds or thousands of specialities. Someone needs to understand all this, and help organizations tap into narrow bands of knowledge. In the health care industry, we are seeing the emergence of "hospitalists," medical professionals who now fulfill the role of steering a patient through the ever increasing complexity that is the world of medical care today. The field is expected to swell from about 15,000 today to 120,000 within a decade. The rise of similar "uber-generalists" is expected in most other industries as well.

Dig beneath any of these trends, and you'll find the birth of billion dollar industries, the emergence of new careers, and all kinds of opportunity!

The Emergence of the Chief Momentum Officer

One of my key themes through the years has been that "faster is the new fast" — that one of the biggest challenges that organizations face is how to keep up with the high-velocity economy.

I'm now observing that in many markets and industries, the pace of change is so fast that we need to put in place a senior executive whose sole area of responsibility is ensuring that the organization can keep up with ever-increasing rates of change.

Organizations need to adapt to all kinds of different issues when it comes to the velocity of change: rapidly changing business models, the emergence of new competitors, ever shrinking product lifecylces, a faster pace of new product development, furious rates of technological innovation, furiously fast new trends in terms of customer interaction, the decreasing shelf-life of knowledge and the more rapid emergence of specialized skills: the list could go on!

Hence, the likely emergence of the new position of "Chief Momentum Officer."

This individual will carry a number of responsibilities, such as:

- managing the product innovation pipeline, so that the organization has a constant supply of new, innovative products, as existing products become obsolete, marginalized, or unprofitable

- managing the talent pipeline, so that the organization has the ability to quickly ingest all kinds of specialized new skills

- managing the technology pipeline, so that the organization can adapt itself to constantly improving and ever-more sophisticated IT tools that will help to better manage, run, grow and transform the business

- maintaining and continually enhancing brand and corporate image; as I've written many times before, brands can become "tired" and irrelevant if they aren't continually freshened and refreshed

- ensuring that the organization is continuing to explore new areas for opportunity, and that it has the right degrees of innovation momentum

- ensuring that the business processes and structure of the organization are fine-tuned on a continuous basis so that it can keep up with all the fast-change swirling around it

- ensuring that a sufficient number of "experiential" programs are underway with respect to product, branding, markets, and other areas so that the overall expertise level of the organization is continually enhanced.

In other words, the CMO has two key responsibilities:

- keeping a fine tuned eye on the trends which will impact the organization in the future, and which will serve to increase the velocity that the organization is subjected to; and

- keeping their hands on the appropriate levers throughout the organization so that it can keep evolving at the pace that these future trends will demand.

I don't know if that makes perfect sense, but I think it's a good issue to think about.

Failing at the Future
Ten Reasons Why
Some Companies Will Miss Out
on the Economic Upturn!

At the height of the economic downturn, I was invited to be the closing keynote speaker at the Missouri Governor Economic Development Congress in St. Louis. It seemed to be a pretty dispirited audience as in many areas of the "Heartland" the region had seen a significant economic contraction. People and organizations were in a mindset that there might not be a lot of economic opportunity in the future. My keynote focused on some of the things that audience members should be thinking about to help them get out of their 'economic rut.'

Just over a year ago, the global economy changed. What has it changed to? What is that next economy?

No one is certain, but what we can be sure of is that many industries will be fundamentally different; business models will continue to evolve at a faster pace; new revenue opportunities will continue to emerge; customer expectations will ramp up in terms of quality and service; we'll see the ongoing emergence of new competitors; product life-cycles will continue to shorten as innovation speeds up; and a lot of transformative change will occur in markets and industries as really innovative people continue to shake up the fundamentals.

So how are companies adapting to these realities?

I'm out on the road working with dozens of organizations. I've seen and have worked with two different types of organizations and leaders. I've seen innovation failures — companies that are stuck in their economic rut, and unable to figure out what to do next — but I've also encountered some real pioneers and fast-movers. They are the innovation leaders — they know they can't panic — they have to go forward by innovating, changing and adapting.

So what's holding the innovation laggards back? I think there are several common attributes:

- **Fear of the unknown.** I still see many organizations who are driven by uncertainty. What happens if our market doesn't recover? What happens if we can't rebuild the top line? What happens if our customers don't start spending again? So much fear and uncertainty causes a form of leadership and organization wide paralysis to set in; they're like deer in the headlights, frozen in time. Avoid that fate – and fast!

- **Inertia is easy.** When confronted by change, many people react by .... doing nothing. When things are uncomfortable, the easiest thing to do to deal with that discomfort is to avoid it. Such thinking causes many organizations and the people within them to fall asleep. They keep doing what they've been doing before the recession, hoping that will carry them forward into our next, different economy. Obviously that can't work, for a whole variety of different reasons.

- **It's easy to avoid tough decisions.** Organizations are faced with a lot of change, in terms of business models, customer expectations, cost pressures, new competitors, and countless other challenges. To deal with any one of these issues requires tough decisions, but in many cases, it's easier to put those decisions off into the future rather than having to deal with them.

- **An unwillingness to confront the truth.** Your product might be out of date; your brand might not be seen as relevant and keeping up to date with fast paced innovation in your marketplace; your sales force might be wildly out of date in terms of their product knowledge; your competitors might have a more efficient cost structure because they made the heavy IT investments that you did not. I could go on, but the point is this: you might have serious systemic problems, and are simply unable or unwilling to focus on fixing them. Have a reality check, and use that as a catalyst for action.

- **A short term focus.** You are still caught up in the economic-downturn hysteria headlines, and don't think about business trends longer than three months. By doing so, you are missing out on the fascinating transformations occurring in many markets and industries, and don't see the key drivers for future economic growth, with the result that you aren't capitalizing on them. Innovative organizations have moved beyond the meltdown, and are already busy positioning themselves for the inevitable long term recovery.

- **A culture that is risk adverse.** So far, you've survived through cautious, careful manoeuvers. Yet the recession has left you naked with that strategy: going forward now requires trying to do a lot of things you haven't done before. You've got a culture that doesn't accept such thinking. Change that — now!

- **Paralyzed by the fear of failure.** Related to your risk aversion is a culture that abhors mistakes. Anyone who errs is shunned; people whisper quietly about what went wrong, and what it might mean. Can that thinking! You should take your failures and put them up on a pedestal. It's more important that you try things out, and learn about this new fast paced, post-recession world, since what worked for you in the past obviously won't work for you in the future.

- **Failure to adapt at fast markets.** I'm dealing with companies that know that constant innovation with top line revenue — which means product and service innovation — is now all about time to market. You've got to have an innovation pipeline that is constantly inventing and reinventing the next revenue driver. What you sold in the past you might not sell tomorrow. How are you going to fix that? By getting into the mindset of the high velocity economy.

- **A refusal or unwillingness to adapt to new methodologies and ideas.** In the manufacturing sector, it's all about manufacturing 2.0 or 3.0 or the next phase. In every industry, there is no shortage of new ideas, methodologies, processes, and fundamental change in terms of how to get things done. Maybe you've closed your mind off to new ideas, with the result that you fail to see how your competitors are rapidly shifting their structure, capabilities, time to market, product line, and other fundamentals. Wake up, we're in the era of the global idea machine. The result is that there is a tremendous amount of transformative thinking out there about how to do things differently. Tune in, turn on, and rethink!

- **A loss of confidence.** This economic downturn has had the effect of causing such widespread damage in various industries that some people and organizations and leaders have lost their faith in the future. They aren't certain they can compete, adapt and change. Perhaps this is the biggest challenge of all to overcome — but you can only overcome it by getting out of your innovation rut and moving forward.

Bill Gates once observed that *"We always overestimate the change that will occur in the next two years and underestimate the change that will occur in the next ten. Don't let yourself be lulled into inaction."*

It couldn't have been put better. What's your choice – to be an innovation leader, aware of where we are going in the future, or an innovation laggard, still mired in short term thinking?

Think growth!

How Future Ready
is Your Organization?

How do you prepare people for the future, if they have no interest in it?

That might seem an interesting question, but I've come to the conclusion, after dealing with hundreds of industries and thousands of executives and professionals, that there are quite a few people out there who love the sentiment once professed by Ogden Nash *"progress is great but it's gone on way too long."*

I've learned that there are two types of business executives: those who think about the future quite a bit and who are very forward-oriented in their thinking. They are very innovative, realistic, creative, and open to new ways of thinking, because they are actively preparing for rapid change in terms of skills, markets and industry fundamentals.

Then there are others who are stuck in the status quo.

Once you get the idea that everything around you is changing at a furious pace, consider doing something about it. This might include doing a 'change-quotient' inventory of your organization.

How do you determine the change-quotient? Focus on these issues:

- **Velocity ratio.** What is the rate of change within your industry? What's the velocity of business model change? How many new competitors are there, and how quickly is the industry blurring as they come into play? What's the staff turnover rate? How quickly do new products come to market?

- **The rate of 'rising tides.'** How quickly are customer expectations changing? If you're in an industry in which there are rapidly rising tides in terms of minimum service delivery, you've got an industry in which there are countless opportunities for innovative, future oriented products and processes.

- **Innovation index.** Is the industry widely innovative, or are there only a few scattered folks who dare buck the current reality? Is everyone in the industry generally stuck in the past, or is there a widespread focus on the future, with a lot of innovative activity as a result?

- **Retirement rate.** Not to be crude, but how many boomers are there hanging around who want the benefits, want the salary, and want the executive responsibility, but don't want to have to do anything to confront change? This, more than anything, can be one of the key measures for change-capability.

- **Generational tolerance.** Out on the speaking circuit, I've been meeting thousands of Gen-X and Gen-Connecters in a lot of industries who scream in silent frustration each and every day. They're stuck in organizations with management who actively work to kill new ideas. They're full of innovation, but they have no outlet for it. On the other hand, there are other industries where the frustration doesn't boil away, but instead, is tapped for opportunity. Spot those industries where "young people" are welcomed as a source for ideas and you've got an industry with massive agility and a high change-quotient.

- **Wisdom wealth.** Boomers need not be change-barriers; indeed, there are some who understand where change is occurring, and who are using their years of experience – often with devastating effect – to spot and capitalize on opportunity. These are some of the most powerful organizations on the planet. They've merged the generations, and are change-masters.

Take the time to look at how quickly the future is coming at us today, and then assess whether you, and the organization you work for, are ready for it.

The Big Secrets of Innovative Organizations!

I've been quite privileged through the years to be able to observe, within my global blue chip client base, some of the fascinating innovation strategies that market leaders have pursued.

What is it they do? Many of them make big, bold decisions that help to frame their innovative thinking and hence, their active strategies. For example, they:

- **Make big bets.** In many industries, there are big market and industry transformations that are underway. For example, there's no doubt that mobile banking is going to be huge, and it's going to happen fast with a lot of business model disruption. Innovative financial organizations are willing to make a big bet as to its scope and size, and are innovating at a furious pace to keep up with fast changing technology and even faster evolving customer expectations.

- **Make big transformations.** I'm dealing with several organizations who realize that structured operational activities that are based on a centuries old style of thinking no longer can take them into a future that will demand more agility, flexibility and ability to react in real time to shifting demand. They're pursuing such strategies as building to demand, rather than building to inventory; or pursuing mass customization projects so that they don't have to compete in markets based on price.

- **Undertake big brand reinforcement.** One client, realizing the vast scope and impact of social networking on their brand image, made an across the board decision to boost their overall advertising and marketing spending by 20%, with much of the increase going to online advertising. In addition, a good chunk of existing spending is being diverted as well. Clearly, the organization believes that they need to make big broad, sweeping moves to keep up to date with the big branding and marketing change that is now underway worldwide.

- **Anticipate big changes.** There's a lot of innovative thinking going on with energy, the environment and health care. Most of the organizations that have had me in for a keynote on the trends that are providing for growth opportunities have a razor sharp focus on these three areas, anticipating the rapid emergence of big opportunities at a very rapid pace.

- **Pursue big math.** Quite a few financial clients are looking at the opportunities for innovation that come from "competing with analytics," which offers new ways of examining risk, understanding markets, and drilling down into customer opportunity in new and different ways.

- **Focus on big loyalty.** One client stated their key strategic goal during the downturn this way: *"we're going to nail the issue of customer retention by visiting every single one in the next three months to make sure that they are happy and that their needs are being met."* Being big on loyalty means working hard to ensure that existing revenue streams stay intact, and are continually enhanced.

- **Focus on big innovation.** One client stated their innovation plan in a simple yet highly motivating phrase: "*think big, start small, scale fast.*" Their key goal is to build up their experiential capital in new areas by working on more innovation projects than ever before. They want to identify big business opportunities, test their potential, and then learn how to roll out new solutions on a tighter, more compact schedule than ever before.

- **Think big change in scope.** One client became obsessed with the innovation strategy of going "upside down" when it came to product development. Rather than pursuing all ideas in house, they opened up their innovation engine to outsiders, looking for more partnership oriented innovation (with suppliers and retailers, for example), open innovation opportunities, and customer-sourced innovation. This lit a fuse under both their speed for innovation as well as their creativity engine.

- **Innovate in a big way locally.** We're in a big, global world, but that doesn't mean that you can't innovate locally. One client in the retail space pursues an innovation strategy that allows for national, coordinated efforts in terms of logistics, merchandising and operations, yet also allows a big degree of freedom when it comes to local advertising, marketing and branding.

- **Share big ideas.** One association client pursued an innovation that was relentless on community knowledge sharing. They knew if they could build an association culture in which, on a regular basis, people shared and swapped insight on how to deal with fast changing markets and customers, that they could ensure their members had a leg up and could stay ahead of trends. Collaborative knowledge is a key asset going forward into the future, and there's a lot of opportunity for creative, innovative thinking here.

- **Are big on solving customers problems.** Several clients have adopted an innovation strategy that is based on the theme, "*we're busy solving customers problems before they know they have a problem,*" or conversely, "*we're providing* *the customer with a key solution, before the customer knows that they need such a solution."* That's anticipatory innovation, and it's a great strategy to pursue.

- **Align strategies to the big bets.** There's a lot of organizations out there who are making "big bets" and linking innovation strategies to those bets. WalMart has bold goals for the elimination of all packaging by a certain date; this is forcing a stunning amount of innovation within the packaging sector. Some restaurants aim to reduce food and packaging waste by a factor of dozens; this is requiring stunning levels of creativity in the kitchen.

These are but a few examples. The essence of the thinking is that we are in a period of big change, and big opportunity comes from bold thinking and big creativity!

Ten Things
You Need to do to
Innovate in a Recession

Business Week ran an article at one point titled "10 Worst Innovation Mistakes in a Recession." I thought it might be better to point out things we should be doing, rather than avoiding -- and wrote this blog as a result.

It's easy to point out mistakes. It can be harder to indicate what you should be doing.

I've been out speaking to organizations about trends, the future, innovation and creativity for over fifteen years. Since last year, when the meltdown began, I've been keynoting events worldwide, rapidly adjusting my theme to one of "how you can innovate during a recession." I've had the opportunity of seeing first hand quite a few very innovative strategies from CEOs and others in a wide variety of events, and I keep modifying my message to incorporate a vast variety of ideas.

Here's a list of 10 off the top of my head:

1. **Focus your team — relentlessly — on growth**. At an event I keynoted not too long ago the CEO of this global organization got on stage before me and spoke about the recession for one minute. He then spent 19 minutes speaking to the growth opportunities that the organization could pursue. That's what everyone needs to do right now. There are growth opportunities in every industry. Focus on them!

2. **Respond faster**. When I keynoted a food industry summit in New York, we spoke of the need to respond faster to the fact that consumer preferences were changing more rapidly than ever before. More people eating at home, sensitive to dollars, looking for food-comfort. Reformulate new brand and product options faster. Just do it. Don't study — do.

3. **Invest in the brand**. Brands can become weaker in a recession, particularly as consumers scramble for value. Decide where you want to reposition your product/brand, and act fast to do it rather than studying it to death.

4. **Mix it up**. Don't assume that what worked before the recession will work now. Try out a lot of ideas, particularly around value. "I'm experimenting rapidly with price points and product mix."

5. **Invest in experience**. Lots of your staff will be down in the dumps, spinning their wheels. Get a message out that NOW is the time to invest in experience. Try things out, to build up the collective experience of your team.

6. **Kill off the innovation killers.** Reframe your team, so that they are thinking "what a great idea," rather than viewing with suspicion any new ideas. Remember — everyone is worried about being laid off, and paranoia sucks the life out of innovation faster than anything else.

7. **Collaborate within the industry**. When I keynoted the American Nursery and Landscape Association event, I stood in awe of the blog they were running that was offering practical,

on the ground, easy to implement ideas that retailers could put into their stores NOW.

8. **Seek ideas**. Go knowledge farming once a day, looking for ideas on customer service, operations, IT strategies, and just about anything else. There's a flood of ideas out there — now's a great time to chase them down and do things.

9. **Partner up**. Sure, resources are scarcer during a recession. That's why you can speed up innovation with anything — from advertising, to customer service, business model implementation, IT strategy, opportunities for operational excellence or just about anything else — by seeking partners to help you out. That will help you achieve key goals faster.

10. **Get over it**. Lots of organizations are still stuck in the anger and denial phase of the Seven Steps of Economic Grief. Make a decision to get into the acceptance stage, and move on. This recession will pass, just like every other one.

These are but a few things you should do when dazzled by uncertainty. The key thing is to be focused on the future, opportunity, and growth. Optimism is critical!

Ten Reasons Why Innovation Matters for Small Business

A while back I did a full day of filming for a small business oriented Website in partnership with Cisco. The video clips would be augmented by a series of articles that focused on the theme of "innovation for small/medium business" (often referred to as SME's!) The morning before I went out for a day of filming, I sat down at my desk and wrote this post which would catch the essence of the video clips for that day.

There are a number of reasons why there is unprecedented opportunity for innovation within the small/medium enterprise sector:

- **The emergence of the contingent workforce**. There has never been a better time for professionals and individuals with specialized knowledge to set up shop, and provide their services to a vast global client base.

- **Complexity drives partnership**. As the high velocity economy evolves, organizations are finding an increased need for solutions to very complex problems; often, the only solution might be a very unique company or individual that is focused on that one particular issue.

- **Opportunity is endless**. Countless new markets, products, and business models are emerging on a continuous basis. Who will sell, support and service these new lines of opportunity?

- **Flexibility is easy**. One of the video clips will tell the story of a wood mouldings manufacturer I spent some time with. Their innovation story, involving how they turned the tables on Home Depot through a logistics innovation, is truly inspiring. You don't have to be a big organization to succeed with innovation, you simply need an open mind and the willingness to change.

- **Lifestyle drives decisions**. I bailed out of the corporate sector, and have been working out of a home office for over 20 years. I have never regretted a moment, and now see a massive trend of people making the same lifestyle decision.

- **Rapid emergence of new markets**. I identified the outdoor living room trend in 2003 — and today, the outdoor living product market is estimated at $15.7 billion, or 37% of total lawn and garden spending. There are a vast number of small and medium organizations who saw the trend unfold, and jumped in. Those types of rapid opportunities will continue to emerge in the future.

- **Lower cost to innovate**. The cost of sophisticated technology continues to drop. SME's today can do things that were the domain of Fortune 500's five years ago. Tomorrow, they'll be the most sophisticated operators on the planet, able to suddenly shift their skills and resources, marketing strategies and campaigns and operating methodology and structure. If they innovate correctly, they can do the things that big business do — but do it better.

- **New careers are emerging**. Think location intelligence professionals, hospitalists and manure managers (yes, seriously.) These are all some of the new careers unfolding before our very eyes. Many new careers can emerge within the structure of the SME economy.

- **It fits the fundamental transformation of business**. There is a new workforce emerging, and SME's are a big part of it. There is plenty of opportunity for skills provision on a global basis as we transition from a 20th century organizational model to the flexible, adaptable, scalable structure of the 21st.

- **The barriers to innovation are fewer**. My experience has taught me that small and medium sized organizations have little of the "organizational sclerosis" that clogs up the structure of their larger, Fortune 5000 cousins. They can adapt and react quickly, and often don't get bogged down in the deadly process of killing innovation with attitudes such as, "you can't do that because we've always done it this way."

I can put some personal perspective on these points. Both my wife and I, successful professionals with bright corporate careers in our futures, stepped out of large global organizations over 20 years ago in order to build our own small, but global business. I often make a joke on stage that "I work really hard to not have to go and get a job" - but that's not really true.

All of the issues above have been key to the success of our own business, and if you adopt them as your own personal mantra, you will really discover that the 21st century really can be the era of massive small business success.

Branding, Marketing & Manufacturing 2.0

I came off a series of keynotes at one point that were focused on social networking, manufacturing, marketing and branding. I pulled together a number of thoughts that I had jotted down on various pieces of paper while preparing for them. It might seem a bit disjointed, but if you study it carefully, you'll find the essence of what many orgnaizations need to be thinking about today.

From a variety of keynotes through the last few weeks, here's what we have got to deal with.

The consumer of today is:

- time challenged

- attention starved

- jumpy and fast with product perceptions

- edgy and vocal when operational excellence is not provided or perceived

- influenced differently in terms of brand/product/service choice

- more vocal when they've been "wronged"

- faster in adopting new trends and ideas.

As a result of this, today's new product is:

- faster to market

- more collaborative in design

- solutions oriented, responding to the fast consumer

- rapidly redefined by the customer

- having to maintain a brand image that is energized and up-to-date.

Combine these two observations, and it means that today's new branding and advertising must be:

- more transformational

- revived and rejuvenated on a more regular basis

- lifestyle oriented

- experimental

- shifting its focus online

- changing faster in terms of message

- going premium and upscale, to avoid commoditization.

The key things to think about when dealing with these new realities are:

- focus on the opportunity that comes from such rapid change, not the threat

- don't panic at the pace

- focus on the value of your product or service

- collaborate with your partners (i.e. packaging companies, retailers, consumer goods companies)

- invest in experiential capital by trying out lots of new ideas

- understand that the pace of change is only going to increase

- transition your team to think differently — innovate!

If I Ran Your Company, Here's What I Would Do!

Supertramp — a band from the 80's — had a minor hit with the song "On the Long Way Home," which featured the memorable line, "when you're up on the stage, it's so unbelievable."

It is, quite. And when you're up there, you realize how lucky you are to be able to share with the audience the wisdom you've picked up by observing some of the world's top innovators.

Recently, after a presentation to an audience of 3,000 people, I was approached by a CEO who was quite inspired by my remarks. He then asked me a fascinating question: "what would you do if you took over the leadership of my company right now?" We chatted for a while and I believe I provided some pretty succinct insight; but since then, I've been thinking about that question. Here's a part of my answer.

Maximize your best revenue opportunities

I'd make sure that any existing revenue relationships remain intact, and then some. I'd work on having my team obsess on growing existing high value customer relationships through service excellence. Let's make sure that we meet their needs. It will likely be easier to keep existing revenue flowing rather than finding new ones, particularly through a time of economic challenge.

Obsess over time to market

I'd work hard to accelerate product innovation; market life-cycles are collapsing, and I'd make sure every member of the team reoriented themselves to that reality. I'd focus on getting R&D to think in terms of faster cycles; I'd ramp up sales force education so that they were better aware of what's coming next. I'd have the team thinking in terms of 3-6-9-12: here's what we will be doing in the marketplace 3, 6, 9 and 12 months from now. I'd layer on top of that some insight into 1-2-5-10: what we might be doing 1, 2, 5 and 10 years from now.

Reduce product costs through process improvement and better project execution

There is no shortage of innovative ideas, structures and concepts involving process and production methodologies. I'd make sure we were looking at finding those who are doing leading edge work in this area, inside or outside our industry, and learn from them.

Reduce structural costs through collaboration

At this point in time, in a global world that allows for instant, smart collaboration among teams, there is no reason for massive duplication of skills and talent throughout an organization. I'd start to rethink those silos, and restructure for a new skills deployment approach. Right off the bat, I'd encourage a few cross-organizational collaboration efforts, to get people used to the idea of tackling fast new problems rather than arguing about structure and hierarchy.

Focus on the pipeline of talent innovation

I've said it before and I'll say it again. The depth of your bench strength is critical to future success. I'd have everyone take a good look at our pipeline, to see if it will meet upcoming needs. If not, I'd get a program in place to fix that fast.

Relentlessly and aggressively chase costs

I'm not talking about spontaneous slash and burn spending cuts: I'd refocus on transitioning the role of staff from tactical efforts to a strategic role. I've spent time with the CIO's and CFO's of some pretty major organizations. All of them have provided in-depth insight onstage during customer panels that have focused on the role of IT in the business to run the business better, grow the business and transform the business. There remain countless opportunities for IT oriented innovation to rip unnecessary costs out of the business, and it involves this tactical to strategic transition.

Enhance quality and reliability of product

Last year, I spoke to 2,500 global quality professionals on the challenges that the high velocity economy presents to the concept of quality. The fact is, new issues are hitting us in the marketplace faster than ever before. The global idea loop means that quality challenges can become a sudden, massive worldwide PR nightmare faster than we've ever been prepared for. That's why avoiding quality problems remains a critical focus. I'd take a look at how well we're dealing with quality issues, and whether we've got the agility to respond in this new world of heightened PR challenges. I'd also have a group prepare an immediate outline of challenges and problems with customer service and satisfaction.

Capture new emerging growth markets faster

I'd begin to orient the team so that we knew about which market opportunities might come next, and then spend time aligning ourselves to innovate faster in such markets. I recently spent some time with one client, and the focus of our discussion was how a new market was set to unfold in the next three months. Expectations were that the market — for a unique consumer product, with potential sales in the billions of dollars — might last for a period of eighteen months, before being eclipsed by the next stage of development. Essentially, the CEO was looking at a situation where they had to figure out how to jump into this new fast market, and make the most of it in an extremely short period of time. That's a new skill structure to wrap an organization around, and one that every organization must learn to master.

*   *   *   *   *

Oh, and one of the first things I'd do? I would immediately convene a senior management/leadership meeting, and bring in a futurist and innovation expert to wake my people up to the potential that can come from energizing ourselves towards future opportunities.

Innovation and the New Workforce

At one point, I was invited in to address 1,000 executives attending the IHRIM (International Human Resource Information Management) professional association annual conference in Houston, Texas. My theme? The future of the workforce. The essence of my keynote revolved around the concept of "ten unique characteristics of 21st Century skills."

Some key drivers which impact organizations today, whether business or government are:

- **velocity** - business is just plain fast, and our workforce must cope with that

- **change capacity** - there's a big disconnect in how quickly some people can deal with rapid change compared to others

- **idea instantaneity** - we're in a new world in which ideas or issues can quickly speed out of control, or work to our advantage

- **knowledgeability** - global insight is increasing at a furious pace, leading to ever larger pools of knowledge

- **innovation opportunity** - rapid rates of discovery lead to massive new opportunities to bring new products and services to market

- **idea discovery** - our interconnected world now allows unique ideas to gain a global audience in a flash

- **consumer spontaneity** - the low attention span consumer is fleeting when it comes to "loyalty to brand"

- **business intensity** - operational excellence is the name of the game, given an economy which simply runs "fast"

- **skills availability** - it is going to be more difficult to access skills.

When we are thinking about deployment of skills we must be thinking about:

- attracting the right skills, at the right time, for the right purpose

- providing for business flexibility in a time of rapid change

- establishing a constantly shifting, evolving "workforce on demand"

- enabling this with sophisticated tools, infrastructure and skills access capabilities.

Innovation and the New Workforce

Messing with Bits of Business Strategy

I've been dealing with a lot of organizations who have had some very interesting, innovative approaches to business strategy. Here's a short list of how to stir up some innovation by messing with your business strategy:

- **Look out.** Don't ask what you can do to run your business better — ask what you can do to run your customer, supplier or partner's business better!

- **Move beyond.** Most projects start out with one strategic goal in mind. Successful innovators realize part way into the project that a myriad of other new, unknown, and very cool opportunities are opening up, ones that they hadn't even thought of before. Keep your eyes open!

- **Turn the tables.** A lot of companies are being WalMartized and HomeDepotized, and have to meet certain operational expectations. Innovators go beyond this, and do cool things

that let them regain more control over the relationship —
usually with projects that give them more information on
what's happening on the shelf than the "big guys" have!

- **Clarify fuzziness.** In the last few years, companies have
found that the reliability of information around chargebacks,
end-cap fee management, promo display management and all
the other esoteric stuff, has become extremely fuzzy, because
they've lost control of the information. They've beat this back
by making financial/accounting reconciliation important once
again. It flows right to the bottom line .... and can be an easy
win.

- **Be cool.** Smart people don't want to work for companies that
have no innovation-oxygen. They're looking for companies that
are busting their markets, ramping up growth, and who are
willing to take a risk. Your brand isn't just your product — it's
your attractability-index! And here's an even better secret: even
existing staff want you to be cool. They're seeing innovation,
and they want you doing it too, even if they grumble and groan
about it.

- **Build your street-cred.** Your customers, suppliers and
partners live in a world in which everyone has instant insight,
operational excellence, and staff who know what is going on.
If you don't, you lose your credibility. You've got to continue
to invest to keep up with the ever increasing minimum-bar-of-
expectations that's out there.

- **Slice and dice.** You're a loser if you play in a commodity
economy. Build the intelligence that lets you know where you
can win by being premium, and toss the rest of your customers
overboard.

- **Routinely innovate.** Lots of companies continue to struggle
with SOX and Rule 404. Few approached it as an innovation
opportunity; but those who did won big, as they got away from
spreadsheet based compliance, and realized real business

process transformation. View any emerging regulatory requirement as an innovation opportunity, and you're golden!

- **Extend and embrace.** Make your insight your partners insight, and let your transactions be their transactions! While "portals" sounds so-90's, it's still one of the leading edge innovation strategies out there, and it has a big impact.

Being Innovative Depends on the Company You Keep!

Many people see a trend and see a threat. Smart people see the same trend and see opportunity.

Think about that statement, and then ask yourself "how do you keep yourself in an innovative frame of mind." A good part of it has to do with the company you keep! I'd suggest that you surround yourself with:

- **optimists -** you need to hang out with people who see all kinds of opportunity – not gloomsters who are convinced there is no future out there!

- **people who do** - action oriented people. Folks who accomplish things. Those that do.

- **people with open minds** - innovators aren't prepared to accept the status quo – they are willing to explore and understand different viewpoints, and use that as a kickoff for creativity.

- **people who have experienced failure** - innovation comes from risk; risk comes from trying things. Try lots of things, and many will fail. That's good. That builds up experience, which gives you better insight into a fast paced world.

- **oddballs and rebels** - some of the most brilliant thinking and best ideas can come from those who view the world through a different lens. They may seem odd at times, but they can be brilliantly creative.

- **good listeners and debaters** - they're willing to challenge ideas, analyze issues, and think through the possibilities.

- **people who think differently than you do** - if you really want to be innovative, go to two conferences a year that have nothing to do with what you do. You'll be amazed at what you learn, and how it will re-stir your creative juices.

In every single keynote I focus on future trends and opportunities, and link that to the process and mindset of innovation. I'm an optimist, continually trying new things, listening to other people, watching, and observing. Most important, I refuse to give in to the pervasive negative thinking that so many people seem to envelope themselves within. Maybe that's why I see so many opportunities in today's economy.

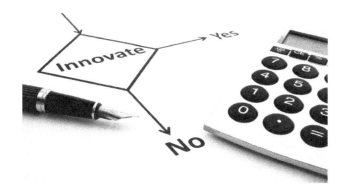

The Importance of Innovation in the High Velocity Economy

What is the shape of the economy as we go forward into a period that involves more high velocity business change? I do know that one answer to this question is this -- the ability of an organization to respond to rapid, relentless, continuous change will increasingly define its future success.

As we climb our way out of a global economy in which change occurred rather slowly, to one that is driven by short, sharp shocks that can completely define markets, competitors, buisness models or customer behavior, it's perhaps a good time for business organizations to ask themselves if they're well positioned for what comes next – whatever that might be!

Are they? I'm not so sure. In the last decade, as a futurist and innovation consultant speaking at countless numbers of global conferences, I've had the remarkable opportunity to spend time with the senior leadership of some of the worlds most innovative, world-class organizations. In doing so, I've witnessed first hand what innovation leaders are doing to ensure that they can survive and thrive in a period of rapid economic change.

What are they focused on?

- **Mastering fast markets.** They're immersed in a world in which product innovations occur so fast that "time to market" is now measured in weeks rather than years.

- **Product innovation.** They're busy ensuring that they have a continual pipeline of new products or services that will generate new revenue as old revenue is displaced.

- **Dealing with disruptive technology.** They're dealing with the fact that a furious pace of technological innovation continues unabated, with the rapid emergence of new technologies that change entire industries. For example, what happens when our cell phones and smart phones become the credit card infrastructure of the future?

- **Customer engagement.** They are involved in rapidly changing the method by which they engage with their customer base and re-energizing their brand, knowing that consumer mindset has become increasingly difficult to capture as the relentless march of social networking technologies continues unabated.

- **Business model innovation.** They are busy innovating with business models, knowing that the only certainty for future success is uncertainty. Consider Wizzit, a South African bank that is based entirely upon the exchange of text messages. That's business model disruption right there!

No matter what type of high velocity change organizations are dealing with, in many cases it comes down to their adaptability and capability to share ideas, collaborate, and form "fast teams" to tackle new opportunities and challenges.

It's not just these areas that they are focused on. They also know that their ability to compete on the global stage requires that they operate with a startling degree of efficiency. They ensure that they have a cost structure that permits them to operate in a world of razor tight margins. They know that their success increasingly comes from the existence of an intelligent, up-to-date network and technology infrastructure that provides the foundation for their innovation engine.

That's the new world of business, and we'd do well to pay attention to it. The reality for many organizations going forward is that they must learn to act and operate at the same high degree of razor-sharp clarity of action as any other global competitors. That means squeezing out every drop of potential efficiency as operating margins become thinner. Managing with continued ongoing cost input volatility, particularly as a result of the wild gyrations in global currency markets. Learning to collaborate and generate innovative insight at blinding speed.

In a nutshell, many companies must operate more efficiently, and learn to compete like global competitors. They need to learn to scale fast, act fast, innovate fast, and compete fast. To do that, they've got to make sure that they've got the necessary foundation in place that allows them to do what the global competition does.

The Importance of Linking Agility and Innovation

Innovative organizations focus on the concept of agility. They can manage fast change, new risk, business market turmoil, staffing challenges, and market commoditization. They can do this because they are relentlessly focused on the future and the trends that will impact them.

They ensure that they innovate and adapt based on rapidly changing circumstances, on a continuous basis. Innovation isn't just about new product; it's an inclusive mindset in which everyone knows that they must stay relentlessly focused on the religion of innovation: how do we do things differently to run the business better, grow the business and transform the business.

How do they do this? By adopting several key guiding principles that form the basis for all corporate strategy and activities going forward:

- **Plan for short term longevity.** No one can presume that markets, products, customers and assumptions will remain static: everything is changing instantly. Business strategies and activities must increasingly become short term oriented while fulfilling a long term mission.

- **Presume lack of rigidity.** Many organizations undertake plans based on key assumptions. Agile organizations do so by presuming that those key assumptions are going to change regularly over time, and so build into their plans a degree of ongoing flexibility.

- **Design for flexibility.** In a world of constant change, products or services must be designed in such a way that they can be quickly redesigned without massive cost and effort. Think like Google: every product and service should be a beta, with the inherent foundation being one of flexibility for future change.

- **Build with extensibility.** Apple understood the potential for rapid change by building into the iPod architecture the fundamental capability for other companies to develop add-on products. Think the same way: tap into the world. Let the customer, supplier, partners and others innovate on your behalf!

- **Harness external creativity.** In a world in which knowledge is evolving at a furious pace, no one organization can do everything. Recognize your limits, and tap into the skills, insight and capabilities of those who can do things better.

- **Plan for supportability.** Customers today measure you by a bar that is raised extremely high. They expect you to deliver the same degree of high-quality that they get from the best companies on the planet. They expect instant support, rapid service, and constant innovation. If you don't provide this, they'll simply move on to an alternative.

- **Revisit with regularity.** Banish complacency. Focus on change. Continually revisit your plans, assumptions, models and strategies, because the world next week is going to be different than that of today.

Simple Guidance to Speed Up Your Team

When everything is faster still, leaders who are intent on mastering the future and riding the opportunities afforded by fast paced trends should focus on these things:

- **Build up experiential capital.** Think big, start small, scale fast. The experiential projects are the "start small" part of the equation. Know what you don't know, and set out to learn those things.

- **Master collaboration and share.** The world is changing too fast, and things are too complex, to do it all on your own. Innovators have mastered the skill of learning from others.

- **Focus on tactical to strategic transitions.** Innovators don't have staff who perform a lot of routine tasks. Each and every single person helps to achieve the core strategic goals of the organization, even if just in a small way.

- **Monitor global idea cycles.** Your future is being invented all around you, and your success comes from your ability to plug in, tune in, and turn on.

- **Fuse generational insight.** We've got really disparate viewpoints, capabilities and levels of patience amongst generations. Innovators bring these differences together in order to get the best from each generation.

- **Take on anticipatory projects.** One thing is certain, tomorrow won't be like today. Innovators look at what might happen tomorrow, and try those things out, in order to be better prepared for when the future arrives.

- **Be a farmer.** It's all about growth, and learning how to have relentless focus on that mission.

- **Displace indecision.** It's simply unacceptable to waver, wait, and pause. Innovators get things done.

- **Implement quicker.** There's not a lot of time to get things done when markets, customers, expectations, competitors and business models all change at a furious pace. Innovators are religious on agility and speed.

- **Think bold.** This isn't a time for small visions and small ideas. We're witnessing the birth of transformative new industries, companies, careers and ideas. Jump on board and go for the big win, not just the small stuff.

In five years, your business, markets, products, customers, industry and structure will look nothing like they do today.

Are you taking the practical steps that will help align your organization for this future?

Innovators Aren't Afraid To Ask Tough Questions!

Innovative people are unafraid to ask questions, they aren't afraid to:

- ask the tough questions

- act on the answers to those tough questions

- ask questions that make people uncomfortable

- challenge others to ask tough questions

- ask why it has become acceptable to not ask questions

- ask questions that challenge fundamental assumptions

- ask questions that show their complete lack of knowledge about something — which is ok

- ask questions that might make their boss unhappy

- indicate that while they don't know the answer to the tough questions, they're prepared to find out

- suggest that maybe there have now been enough questions, and something must be done in order to move forward.

What's the key to this line of thinking?

Organizations can become too comfortable with routine, and unless this is challenged on a regular basis, complacency becomes a killer. By constantly putting a whole bunch of tough questions on the table, innovators can ensure that innovation paralysis does not set in.

Innovation: Think Big, Start Small, Scale Fast!

A key innovation message that I suggest my clients focus on involves the concept of "thinking big, starting small, and scaling fast."

What does the message imply:

- **Think big.** Identify the long term transformative trends that will impact you. These could include significant industry change, business model disruption, the emergence of new competitors, product or service transformation; anything. Essentially, you need to get a good grounding in the "big changes" that will impact your future over a five or ten year period.

- **Start small.** From those trends, identify where you might have weaknesses in skills, products, structure, capabilities, or depth of team. Pick a number of small, experiential orientated projects to begin to fill in your weak points, and learn about what it is you don't know. This will give you better depth of insight into what you need to do in order to deal with the transformative trends identified above.

• **Scale fast.** From those small scale projects, determine which areas need to be tackled first in terms of moving forward more aggressively with the future. Develop the ability to take your 'prototyping' of skills enhancement from the small scale projects into full fledged operations.

It sounds simple, but it's extraordinarily complex. Having said that, it does give you and your team a good conceptual framework for innovation, and orienting yourself to the trends which will provide you with the greatest opportunities and challenges in the years to come.

Bold Beats Old, Fast Beats Big and Other Key Issues

It was a busy fall, with keynotes and leadership events for the likes of PPG, the Utah League of Cities and Towns, St. Joseph's Health Center, Transcontinental Media, the Ohio League of Bankers, the Illinois League of Financial Institutions, the Minnesota Hospital Association CEO Summit, Allied Solutions and many others.

Although each event was a different industry there are several key common themes that all of the senior executives need to focus on:

- **Fast beats big.** We have never lived in a period of time that has involved such rapid change with business models, competitive landscapes, product and service innovation, challenging consumers, a new political dynamic, and countless other new realities. World class innovators are those who move fast, get things done, and keep getting things done.

- **Bold beats old.** All around you right now, there are countless numbers of people and organizations who are out to mess up your business model. They're making bold steps, aggressive moves, and big decisions. This is not a time for timidity; it's a time for BIG ideas and the pursuit of the offbeat.

- **Velocity trumps strategy.** Careful strategic planning can be a critical step in adapting to the future, but in some areas, things are happening so fast that you can't take the time to strategize: you just need to jump in and go. That's experiential capital, it's one of the most important investments that you need to be making now. Understand what it is, and why you need to be investing in it NOW.

- **Flexibility beats structure.** Successful innovators have mastered the ability to form fast teams: they know that their ability to quickly scale resources to tackle fast emerging opportunities or challenges are the only way that they can win in the future. They avoid the organizational sclerosis that bogs too many organizations down.

- **Disruptors destroy laggards.** Step into any industry, and there are people who are busy messing about with the fundamental business models which have long existed. Start your own disruption before you find yourself disrupted.

- **Connectivity is the new loyalty.** With the forthcoming dominance of mobile technology in everyday lives, everything you know about customer relationships is dead. Right now, it's all about exploring and building new relationships throughout the mobile data cloud in which the customer lives. If you don't get that, your brand is dead.

- **Location is the new intelligence.** With connectivity comes location, which results in new applications, business models, methods of customer interaction, and just about everything else. If you don't have a location strategy for your business, you really don't understand how quickly your world is changing around you.

Innovation:
We Need to Suck Less

I'll often be lined up for a conversation with the CEO of a client organization when I'm preparing for a private client CEO leadership/innovation keynote. It's part of a careful diplomatic dance to ensure that my keynote addresses the key issues and challenges that they, as an organization, need to focus on .

During the conversation, I often prepare a summary list of the issues that they put on the table. I've got dozens of scribbled notes from such conversations. Here's one that I just came across. The CEO of this Fortune 1000 organization (obviously, not named) outlined some of the key themes that I needed to address. As he put it, "we need to:"

- **increase our bench strength** - we don't seem to have the right skills and the right capabilities at the right time for the right purpose. We need to get better at our skills mix and agility if we are to max out our creative capabilities

- **institutionalize learning** - we tend to fall behind and miss opportunities because our people don't know enough about what is going on "out there"

- **grow high value customer relationships** - we could get much better in solving customers problems before they know they have a problem. If we could do that, we could extend existing revenue faster

- **accelerate product innovation** - we're slow. By the time we get to market, our competitor has already been there. We need to speed things up

- **have a better talent pipeline** - we've got a lot of "dead wood" lying around, performing a lot of tactical, non-strategic work. We need to ensure that we are developing/ingesting new talent faster, for the faster emergence of new issues

- **reduce our structural costs through collaboration** - simply put, there is simply too much duplication of effort. It's the era of social networks; why can't we be "social" internally?

- **suck less** - there's still huge opportunity to reduce product costs through process innovation and better project execution. (yes, he did use this phrase)

- **scale faster** - we really, really need to get better at identifying and capturing growth markets

- **plug knowledge gaps** - there's lots to learn about things we don't know about. We need to invest more in risk oriented projects. We have to fail faster.

What's fascinating about these conversations is that the CEO knows the challenges that need to be addressed; my role is to help to build a message for the team to get them to focus on what they really need to do to become innovation heros.

The simple list above — and this is but one of dozens of such summaries — gives a bit of insight into how you can take innovation beyond simple product oriented innovation.

Remember – innovation is all about answering the questions: "What can I do to run this business better? What can I do to grow this business? And what can I do to transform the business!"

Major 10 Year Trend
Silicon Valley to Control
Future of Every Industry

The next big areas of growth will come from the transformative change that occurs as Silicon Valley comes to drive the pace of innovation in almost every industry - auto, health care, manufacturing, energy, banking, etc. As it does so, it will speed up the rate of innovation.

The impact of this trend is that it will also shift control from any particular industry to the technology companies. The result will be massive business model disruption as new, faster, more nimble competitors who understand technology based disruption, cast aside their slower, ingrained counterparts.

The future belongs, in other words, to those who are fast. Tech companies and tech based innovators certainly understand this! The key issue is speed. Apple, for example, could innovate much faster with new credit card financial systems than any bank could. Google and its tests of automatic car navigation technology will certainly evolve faster than any auto company in Detroit, Japan or Germany could. Unless leaders in those organizations increasingly learn to focus on speed as a metric, and fast-innovation as a core capability, they will loose control of their innovation agenda.

Consider just a few of the trends:

- Banks and credit companies risk losing control of their future as our mobile devices, cell phones and iPhones become credit cards.

- The energy and home construction industry will be impacted as people start to use new personal energy management infrastructure, in the form of devices such as the NEST Thermostat.

- Health care will be transformed by medical device connectivity and bioconnetivity allowing hospitals and nursing homes to extend the reach of their medical professionals to an increasing number of remote locations.

- The auto industry will face tremendousness change as an intelligent highway infrastructure emerges at the same time as intelligent, self-guiding cars and trucks become a regular part of our daily world.

- The world of insurance will be upended as we head to a world of predictive insurance modelling through the use of sophisticated technologies such as on-board GPS devices which monitor driver behaviour.

These are but just a few examples. I can go into any industry today and point out how Silicon Valley and technology is going to cause significant change and upheaval within the industry.

There are many smart executives who understand this trend and realize that right now is the time for aggressive innovation and big thinking. Unfortunately there are many others where this observation passes right over their heads.

Agriculture 2020! Innovation, Growth and Opportunity

One of the events I keynoted was for a small corporate conference that featured what were probably the top 100 cattle, stockyard and feedlot operators in the US. Some of these individuals represented ranches with upwards of 30,000 to 50,000 head of cattle.

My role? To encourage this group to think about future trends in the world of agriculture and food production; opportunities for innovation; and how to live out on the edge in terms of thinking about big ideas.

Real innovation doesn't come from plugging into Twitter, getting onto Facebook or other social medias. It comes from studying obvious future trends, and aligning yourself to those trends to seize opportunity and achieve growth.

It was a thrill to speak to such an exclusive group — and I had a lot of ground to cover! After all, as I pointed out, they've suffered from: stagnant growth (6.4% over 25 years) while imports have tripled; a continuing drop in the number of feedlots; consolidation of buyers (top 4 meat packers control 80% of market from 36% in 1980), which give them fewer options; and an overall decline in consumption in the U.S. (94.3 lbs per capita to 59.1lbs from 1976 to today).

What's the result of these trends, and the impact of the recent recession? Aggressive indecision!

> "Many ranchers are wary of investing in expanding their herds, even with exports rising and prices climbing, because they're uncertain about the future," said Gregg Doud, chief economist at the National Cattlemen's Beef Association, which represents ranchers and feedlots.
> *Where's the Beef: Food Inflation Fears, Wall Street Journal, August 2010*

Yet given this uncertainty, what are the trends that drive the opportunity for innovation? Here's a few.

There is massive, significant opportunity for global growth.

The statistics are simple and clear: the world's population will increase 47%, to 8.9 billion, by 2050; a simple fact - global agriculture production must double to sustain growth; a stark reality - little new arable land will come to play a role in that production. In other words, existing producers will have to double production to keep up with global demand.

Clearly, a substantial number of people are entering the global middle class through the next decade; as noted by McKinsey & Company "Almost a billion new consumers will enter the global marketplace in the next decade .... with an income level that allows spending on discretionary goods."

As this transition to middle class occurs, entire societies will transition to a diet that involves more consumption of meat. In India, the #1 "aspirational purchase" is a television. What do you think is #2? If you said a car, you are wrong — it's a refrigerator!

And right now, refrigerators have only a 13% market penetration! Talk about opportunities for growth.

The opportunity is clear – per capita meat consumption growth from 2000 to 2030 will be 49% in China, 79% in India, and 22% in Brazil.

There are significant long term trends that will drive global agricultural innovation and opportunity, if approached from the right perspective.

Four key trends that will have a huge impact on agriculture from every single perspective are: food security will become an issue of "national interest;" there will be significant international agricultural investments; sustainability practices will move to the forefront of the customer agenda; food quality and safety ratings will become commonplace.

On the first issue – we are going to witness many nation states working fast to ensure the security of their food supply. We are seeing it happen now with China, in order that it can ensure a sustainable reliable supply of food for its population in the future. How big of an issue is this?

> Food security will be the greatest challenge to civilization this century, with shortages leading to higher prices, political instability and mass migration, warn scientists, farmers and academics.
> *Looming food crisis showing on our shelves, Sunday Age, April 2011*

The issue of food security leads to the second big trend - international agricultural investments. Quite simply, there's a lot of investment money sloshing around involving agriculture.

> The World Bank reported this month that the number of large-scale farmland deals in 2009 amounted to about 45 million hectares, compared with an average of less than 4 million hectares each year from 1998 through 2008.
> *Investors bet the farm, Los Angeles Times, September 2010*

Even Harvard University is getting into the act, with a significant investment into one of the biggest ranches in New Zealand — the Big Sky Dairy Farm in Central Otago. (*New Zealand Herald, June 2010*)

These two trends are unfolding at the same time that sustainability practices moves to the forefront of the customer agenda. Consider a very unique partnership between some "unlikely allies" that involve sustainable business practices in agriculture. This is going to affect EVERYONE in the industry:

> Food manufacturers, retailers and WWF are joining forces to address how to feed the world's population, writes Paul Myers. When the World Wildlife Fund engages the ideologically distant interests of the cattle industry, Coca-Cola and McDonald's to discuss global food production, it's clear something is cooking.....
> *Unlikely alliance, Sydney Morning Herald, February 2011*

What is cooking is an effort by these organizations to move sustainability practices to the forefront, in order to respond to consumer demand. And what the sustainability trend leads to is a world in which food quality and safety ratings become commonplace.

> Wal-Mart, which sells more than 20 per cent of all U.S. groceries, is developing an eco-labelling program that will give a green rating to all items sold in its 7500 stores worldwide.
> *Unlikely alliance, Sydney Morning Herald, February 2011*

This will trickle right down to the farm and the ranch. Agriculture is going to have to demonstrate sustainability at a micro-level:

> A group of cattle producers in Gippsland, Victoria, is marketing beef sourced from properties with independently audited environmental management systems that comply with the international ISO 14001 standard. Their "enviromeat beef," sourced from 15 suppliers, is thought to be the first labelled food product backed by

an environmental management system in Australia.
Unlikely alliance, Sydney Morning Herald, February 2011

Many farmers and ranchers might view these issues as a challenge, and a threat. But as I emphasized in my keynote, some people see a trend and see a threat, others see opportunity! The key innovation opportunity is to know how to work within these new realities in order to stay ahead of what the customer demands!

Ranchers need to think big! There are huge transformative opportunities!

In my keynotes, I always try and challenge the team to adapt to the mindset of Bill Gates, who observed that "we always overestimate the change that will occur in the next two years and underestimate the change that will occur in the next ten."

I always pull out a number of examples of some of the big, bold, whacky innovative thinking that is occurring in any particular industry.

I've long observed that one of the key global economic drivers is that a lot of people are spending a lot of time solving the big problems faced by the industrialized world. What's likely to lead us out of this recession? A combination of bold goals on energy and the environment, significant investment in health care to fix a system that is set for absolutely massive challenges, combined with high-velocity innovation in all three sectors.

In the spirit of that observation, think about this report!

America's dairy farmers could soon find themselves in the computer business, with the manure from their cows possibly powering the vast data centers of companies like Google and Microsoft.....With the right skills, a dairy farmer could rent out land and power to technology companies and recoup an investment in the waste-to-fuel systems within two years, Hewlett-Packard engineers say in a research paper to be made public on Wednesday...According to H.P.'s calculations, 10,000 cows could fuel a one-megawatt data center, which would be the equivalent of a small computing center used by a bank.

"The cows will never replace the hydroelectric power used by a lot of these data centers," Mr. Kanellos said, "But there is interest in biogas, and this presents another way to make manure pay." *One moos and one hums, but they could help power Google, New York Times, May 2010*

Whacky? Crazy? Who is to say! I actually wrote about this opportunity back in 2004 when I penned my "I found the future in manure" article!

Innovators concentrate on all kinds of innovation opportunities.

I've always stressed that people can challenge themselves to innovate by focusing on 3 key questions; what can we do to run the business better, grow the business, and transform the business.

In that context, for these ranchers, there's plenty of innovation opportunity. When it comes to running the business better, there is a massive opportunity for the continued deployment of technology to better manage the herd; deal with food safety and traceability issues; manage the health of the herd; the list is endless! Growth of the business? Consider the opportunities that come about with direct-to-consumer relationships as our world of connectivity continues to expand. Transform the business? Change the business model! One Australian group was faced with the challenge of getting fresh meat to Indonesia — and so they built the MC Becrux — basically a floating stockyard for thousands of head of cattle! (I admit, to go forward this will have to be done to fit into the sustainability model....)

Innovators ride accelerating rates of change.

Quite simply, there's a lot of scientific driven innovation in the agricultural sector. One conference I spoke at noted these tools that would transform the industry: advances in genomics; combinatorial chemistry; high throughput screening; advanced formulation; environmental science and toxicology; precision breeding; crop transformation; nanotechnology; synthetic biology and bio-informatics; and many more.

It couldn't be said better. Even the field of animal genomics is evolving at a furious pace — the same trend in which Moore's law is driving down the cost of sequencing the human gene, so too it is with animal genetics, which has a big potential impact on the quality of future production.

Innovators adapt to accelerating generational change.

Perhaps the biggest trend occurring in agriculture today is that we are seeing a generational turnover. As the family farm and industrial ranch transition from the baby boomer to today's 25-30 year olds, there will be more rapid ingestion of new technologies. Quite simply, we are going to witness more change on the farm and ranch in the next ten years than we have seen in the last 50! That's providing even more opportunity for innovation!

The Future of Retail Franchise Operations!

One of my recent events was to keynote a multi-unit franchise conference. The audience were owners and operators of multiple franchise operations, primarily from the restaurant/food sector, but also from other franchise operations in auto, pet care, home supplies and other retail product lines.

My keynote topic was built on the theme "Where Do We Go From Here? Why Innovators Will Rule in the Post-Recession Economy – And How You Can Join Them!"

What did I take a look at? A wide variety of the fast-paced trends impacting the retail/restaurant sector today. I broke my talk down into 3 key trends:

• Consumer velocity

• Mobile madness

• Intelligent technology and infrastructure.

Consumer behaviour shifts faster today than ever before.

"The average consumer scans 12 feet of shelf space per second." That's a stat I've long used to emphasize that the attention span of the typical shopper of today is shorter than ever before. Retailers need to innovate to ensure they can keep the attention of today's consumer.

It's not just keeping up with fleeting attention spans — it's about adapting to the fast pace of how quickly consumer choice changes. Consider what is happening with the rapid emergence of revenue in the 'late night' business segment – it was up 12% in the 4th quarter of 2010, compared to only a 2-3% increase for other parts of the day. That's why major chains have been focusing on new "happy hour" offerings — and so their success increasingly comes from how quickly they can scale and adapt to fast moving trends.

We've seen plenty of fast innovation from various organizations in the sector to respond to quick consumer change. Morton's The Steakhouse capitalized on the new consumer sensitivity towards value when it jumped on the trend that involves the "casualization of fine dining" with its $6 mini-cheeseburger.

Other fast trends drive the industry. *The Sydney Morning Herald* ran a great article in April of 2011, noting that "... the world of cooking and restaurants is becoming more like an arm of show business ....." with the result that "everyone wants to see the chef." That's why we are seeing many restaurants from fine-dining to fast casual moving the kitchen to the "front of the house," or in other cases, a lot of TV display technology that provide for video links from tables to the kitchen. The evolution that is occurring is that the chef is becoming the star, and more and more of the staff are becoming 'performers.' Innovators in appropriate sectors would see the opportunities and jump on this trend.

Whatever the case may be, the consumer of today changes quickly, and innovators check their speed and agility in being able to respond to this reality.

Technology – especially mobile technology – has become the key influencer of today's consumer decision making

Simply put, the velocity of mobile adoption, local search and product promotion is evolving at a pace that is beyond furious. Consider the growth rates underlying today's technology. It took two years for Apple to sell two million iPhones. It took two months for them to sell two million iPads! It took one month to sell one million iPhone 4's!

The impact of such trends is an explosive rate of growth of wireless Internet usage. Mobile represented but 0.2% of all Web traffic in 2009. That grew to 8% by 2010, and is expected to hit 16% of all traffic this year.

Some suggest that mobile searches now exceed the number of computer based searches. What is also well known is that most mobile searches are for "local content." Not only that, but Google has found that when someone gets a smartphone, the number of searches they make increases 50 times!

What is clear is that people are using their mobile devices to find nearby stores, retailers, restaurants and just about everything else. Combine this with the emergence of new promotion opportunities (through apps and other tools) and you've got a revolution in the making in terms of local product promotion. That's why the success of many retailers/restaurants will come from their success with location-sensitive coupon technology.

Bottom line? Innovation is: rethinking in-store uplift in terms of new methods of interaction!

We will have far more opportunity for operational innovation through the rapid emergence of new intelligent technology, infrastructure and other trends

Consider how quickly near-field payment technology is going to steamroller the retail/restaurant sector. Simply put, over the next few years, the credit cards in our wallet will disappear as our iPhones, Blackberries and Android phones become the credit card infrastructure of the future. This is a HUGE trend — it provides countless opportunities for innovation, disruptive business model change, new competitors, and all kinds of other fun opportunities.

The trend has enormous velocity – we can expect $113 billion in transactions by 2016, with 3.5 billion transactions – and with this comes new opportunities for loyalty and contact followup. From an innovation perspective, the sector will have to ensure they can ingest the new infrastructure quickly enough, and keep on top of the industry change that it will cause to ensure that challenges are turned into opportunity.

There are all kinds of other areas of fast change that present opportunity. Consider the issue of 'green buildings' and sustainability. The *West Australian* newspaper recently noted that "with the rapid increase in knowledge, skills and availability of materials, costs have fallen. The industry now understands how to build green and building a 5-star Green Star building is now generally cost neutral."

Some franchisees are taking this to heart, with aggressive plans involving eco-friendly buildings. Chick-fil-A has a LEED initiative in building a test model restaurant that has water usage down by 40% through rainwater collection; an electricity reduction of 14% through the use of skylights and energy efficient appliances; 20% of the building content is from recycled material; and 30% more fresh air than regular buildings. While the structure is 15% more expensive to build, they expect a fairly quick payback — and they will manage to get a branding image to their customer base that they don't just talk sustainability – they do it!

From this perspective, innovation is keeping ahead of and planning for hyper-innovation with IT, energy, environmental and other infrastructure trends that impact facilities or the nature of the customer interaction.

*   *   *   *   *

I also emphasized that innovators aren't afraid to make bold moves. Every franchise and retail organization today is looking for opportunities for cross-promotion, cross-selling and product placement. So consider this observation from the *Dallas Morning News* in March 2011 in an article titled: *Funeral home adds little sip of heaven: Starbucks Coffee.*

> At McKinney's Turrentine Jackson Morrow Funeral Home, it's now possible to pay your respects to the dead or plan your own funeral with a venti Caramel Macchiato in hand.

Craziness, or smart niche-marketing? I think it's innovation! Consider these other examples.

Many might hold themselves back from Facebook advertising because the concept might simply seem overwhelming for a small to medium sized mulit-unit franchise operation. Yet, today Facebook accounts for 1 of every 3 online ads. And we are seeing the rapid emergence of new online 'aggregators' that are focused on helping small business take advantage of that fact. These organizations — such as Blinq — manage the buying of thousands of individualized ads, based on age, location, interests.

Buffalo Wild Wings gave mobile promotion a shot for one recent NFL based initiative, and indicated that they tripled the return on their investment.

Think differently in terms of new ways of reaching the consumer. Pizza Pizza, a Canadian chain, recently released a new iPhone App that allows online ordering. Nothing new or special about that – such apps are becoming a dime a dozen, and are quickly becoming de rigueur. What is cool is that the chain has revealed that it is working to link the app payment system to university meal card plans, in recognition of the fact that many students in the target market might not have credit cards (or "credit worthy" cards.)

Bottom line? There's a lot going on, and a lot to figure out. We should just get out, get involved, explore the fascinating new world that surround us! Try new ideas, explore new initiatives, undertake new projects. One of the only ways to get ahead is to work quickly to build up your experience in all the new opportunities that surround you.

Ten Enemies
of Innovation!

I had a conference call with a client to discuss an upcoming leadership meeting; I'll be helping the organization think about some of the barriers they have towards innovation, and what they need to do to overcome these challenges.

As we were talking, I scribbled down a short list of some of the issues that I was identifying with them.

- **Tradition.** Some organizations are too caught up with the past, which causes them to lose sight of opportunities for the future.

- **Culture**. Often corporate culture can be stifling, if not deadening. Some build up an organizational sclerosis which eventually clogs up their ability to try to do anything new.

- **Organizational memory.** It causes people to focus on the past instead of the future.

- **Bureaucrats.** Their job is simply to shut down ideas, get people to fill out forms, and reduce the everyday work experience to a series of mind-numbing tasks.

- **Stock markets.** They cause too many senior executives to spend their time thinking about short term hits that can keep the stock price up, rather than working on the big bets that can provide for transformative opportunities. No wonder so many organizations are going private!

- **Job descriptions.** They reduce the role of people to a narrowly defined set of activities and small goals. I've encountered few organizations where innovation success is actually enshrined into the job description, let alone the HR reward system.

- **Mission statements.** They can be a great thing to give everyone an overall sense of purpose. On the other hand, most organizations don't update and refresh them, which means that in many cases, the mission statement has nothing to do with what the organization actually needs to be doing.

- **Strategic planning.** Some organizations get so caught up in the process of strategic planning that they never get beyond the planing stage. Where do you think the phrase "analysis paralysis" comes from — organizations who are busy analyzing things as part of their planning process!

- **Lone wolves.** They're often folks who can lead innovation, since they can have the brilliant ideas that are the spark for greatness. On the other hand, they can become so blinded by their belief that they refuse to accept the ideas and insight of anyone else, forgetting that collaboration is often at the root of all great innovations.

That's a short list of some of the enemies of innovation. Try to take a quick audit of your organization to see how many might be surrounding you and start to plot a strategy in order to deal with the threat that they can present!

What Are Some of the Trends in the Year to Come?

Here are some of the most important trends which will play out in the year to come.:

- **Biz competes again.** North American and Western European companies have lived with constant fear, with the rapid rise of China, the BRIC countries and the N11 on the world stage. And yet, we're now witnessing a scene from the movie 2010: "HAL-9000 – 'What's going to happen?' DAVE – 'Something wonderful'." My sense is that a wide variety of industries, from agriculture to manufacturing to industrial design have been going through a renaissance of thinking in the last few years, and have learned what they need to do to re-innovate, grow again, and aggressively return to local and global markets.

- **The rise of the tinkering economy.** The future is once again being built in the garage next door. But this time, it's the hyper-connected, innovation oriented tinkering economy which is driving things forward. Get used to phrases like "micro factories," "hobby designers" and "personal factories." The future of design, business and manufacturing is being reinvented at collaborative idea factories such as Ponoko, Etsy and eMachineShop.com. There's a revolution underway which is being driven by a globally connected, creatively driven new generation of hobbyists, and the impact is going to be massive!

- **Relationships change.** Everywhere around us, the relationship that we have in our lives with the things that surround us is, well, changing. Our relationship with food is changing as mobile technologies come to influence what we buy, how we shop, and how we track our food intake. Our relationship with our body is undergoing a change as we come to use those same mobile technologies to monitor our diet, track our blood pressure and other vital signs. Our relationship with clothing is changing as embedded technology becomes a part of what we wear — think about GPS enabled shoes for Alzheimer's patients and Zephyr's smart-clothing — which can be used by athletes to track their performance. When relationships change, everything changes, and opportunities for growth and innovative thinking abound!

- **Generational re-generation.** Everywhere we look, there's a massive generational turnover underway, with a change in ownership of organizations from slow moving change adverse baby-boomers to a younger generation that inhales change as a form of innovation oxygen. As family farms and ranches are passed on from father to son and daughter, the rate of adoption of new farming and herd management ideas takes on a greater degree of speed. As older doctors and nurses who were weaned on the paper-heavy patient file head into retirement, they are being replaced by new medical residents who are arriving in the clinic, operating room and by the hospital bed with their iPads, ready to plug in! A shift from change-aversion to change-is-the-greatest-drug is a trend that will speed up our world even more!

- **Revenue reinvention.** Every company is coming to face the reality that they have to become just like Apple in order to survive. The fact that Apple generates over 60% of its revenue from products that didn't exist four years ago might today be an aberration, but given the increasing velocity of business cycles, product innovation, the arrival of new business models, changing customer expectations, the impact of social networks and a series of other trends, soon every organization will find itself in a reality in which constant, relentless reinvention of its product or service line will be crucial to their future success.

- **The dominance of design.** We're on the edge of a massive new era of creativity, with a trend that we might even call the 'iPad-ization of Life.' All one has to do is look at the new NEST thermostat to realize that a new generation of brilliant creativity is about to remake our world. We're not doomed to a future in which everything around us is going to look just like it did in the past — Apple's design influence is quickly going to impact everything around us — from the cars we drive to the lamps we use to the fridges we open to the buses we catch. Clean, simple, easy interfaces and crisp, cool lines. But it's not just the looks — it's the fact that with this new era of design comes intelligence. Our future is going to look great, be intelligent and interactive!

- **Chip-velocity!** Moore's law used to apply only to the computer industry. Yet the rule that the processing power of a computer chip doubles every year while its cost cuts in half is taking on new meaning, as your phone becomes a credit card, your car watches how well you drive on behalf of your insurance company, and your clothing talks to your doctor! All of a sudden, in the era of relentless, pervasive connectivity, innovation in every single industry speeds up when Silicon Valley takes over the innovation agenda!

- **Life beyond politics.** While the U.S. Presidential election and political turmoil will dominate the headlines for 2012, a new generation of leaders are focused on BIG THINKING, BIG IDEAS, and BOLD MOVES. There's a realization that political gridlock is the new normal, whether it's the Democrats and Republications staring each other down, or France and Germany looking at Italy and Greece with a mystified sense of stunned confusion. So while politicians fail to get things done, innovative organizations are casting their mind to the future trends which will really provide opportunity in the future. It's fascinating — the future is back in vogue again! The thinking that is driving it is that we aren't going to fix the problems of the future by doing what we've done in the past. If we do things differently that's how we'll discover the next big opportunity. This is the new mindset driving activities in the world of energy, the environment and healthcare!

- **Leading locally.** There's something odd going on — as the world gets global, we're all going local. We're seeing it with sustainability and local foods; angst and anger at banks and moves to credit unions; and a new volunteerism – as unemployment grew to 7.6%, volunteer service grew by 16%! We're seeing it with local business – a University of Pennsylvania study found that areas with small, locally owned business (<100 employees) had greater per capita income growth than those with the presence of larger, non-local firms! There's a new focus on local co-ops — with more than 100 million people employed worldwide in some type of local co-op. That's why it's fitting that 2012 is the International Year of the Cooperatives, a business model that has stood the test of time for over 150 years. Where ever you look, while we are thinking global, we're acting local!

- **Strategy re-dos.** The impact of all these trends? Executives quickly coming to realize that what they've been doing in the past isn't going to move them forward into the future. It's time to throw out all the old assumptions and try things that are new!

Here's to an exciting year!

Big Food Industry Trend:
Bold Goals, Big Bets

Health, wellness and food are set to become even more linked than ever before.

That's a significant trend that I'm witnessing right now through the various keynotes and consultations that I do with a large range of food/restaurant/consumer product companies, as well as the keynotes I do for major health care groups worldwide. I get to see what food companies are focused on; I get to see what healthcare groups and governments are worried about.

In a nutshell, here's what's happening:

- the importance of health and wellbeing on a global, national, political and healthcare system perspective is accelerating. We've got a big global problem, and nations and governments are racing to deal with it;

- the result is that there is a very significant effort by food companies to speed up their innovation engine with respect to their health and wellness product line – it's being done to mitigate potential political risk down the road;

- it's also being done because it makes increasing business sense — as consumers worldwide begin to adjust their lifestyle, including their food intake, revenues of the health/wellness product line soars. One report suggests, the sale of health and wellness oriented foods is expected to quadruple through the next five years;

- to help accomplish that, food and consumer product companies are making an increasing number of BIG BETS involving product development, and through even more vigorous M&A activities, that enhance their health and wellness product lines.

Making BIG BETS involves establishing big goals. Consider just two examples of "BIG BET thinking:"

- Frito-Lay, the biggest U.S. seller of salty snacks, is embarking on an audacious plan. By the end of the year, it intends to make half its snacks sold in the U.S. with only natural ingredients. *You Put What in This Chip? 24 March 2011, The Wall Street Journal*

- Pepsi intends to grow a $10 billion health and wellness portfolio to $30 billion by 2020 *www.pepsico.com*

Savvy food companies know that globally, they face increasing national, financial, political and healthcare risk. Quite simply, the world is getting fat, people are getting sick, and countries are not going to be able to afford the care for those suffering from the resultant lifestyle disease.

It's the lifestyle disease that provides the biggest challenge in terms of scope. According to the Karolinska Institute, Stockholm, 1.6 billion adults are overweight or obese worldwide and over 50 per cent of adults in the U.S. and Europe fit into this category. With the resultant impact:

> "The number of adults with diabetes worldwide has more than doubled since 1980 to 347 million, a far larger number than previously thought and one that suggests costs of treating the disease will also balloon."
> *Global diabetes epidemic balloons to 350 million, Reuters Health E-Line, June 27, 2011*

The challenge with the lifestyle disease isn't restricted to the Western world; the statin (cholesterol) drug market in China, India and other "BRIC" countries is set to grow at rates of up to 25% compounded per year. In other words, developing nations are soon to see the same lifestyle diseases which are currently sweeping through North America and Europe.

Given this reality, and the economic volatility in Europe, the U.S., Japan and elsewhere as government revenue declines and spending soars, we are going to see far more aggressive efforts by politicians and governments to reign in health care spending, including that related to lifestyle disease. Nations simply can't afford what is set to come in terms of spending.

Much of this activity will come to involve far more aggressive efforts concerning preventative health care programs, including wellness and lifestyle management. We can expect governments and politicians to become far more aggressive with food companies when it comes to their food offerings.

There is a big political risk here on a global scale.

The result? Smart food companies are making BIG BETS right now to grow their health and wellness product lines. It makes great sense from a business prospective; it's critical in order to stay one step ahead of government trends in order to mitigate risk.

So how will food companies grow their health and wellness line of business? By accelerating internal innovation into health and wellness product lines, but also through some pretty aggressive M&A activity. A report by Deloitte suggests that this will include increased M&A activity in dairy, juice, health snacks and functional foods.

Gerald Abelson, president of the Canadian corporate finance group, MNC Multinational Consultants, recently observed in a discussion about global M&A activity in the food and consumer product sector in 2012 and beyond, that "health and wellness is definitely where you want to be in the next three to five years."

Bold Goals – Big Bets!

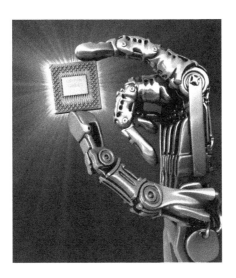

When Silicon Valley
Takes Over
Health Care Innovation

When looking at future health care trends, you need to do so without taking a look at the political issue of health care reform. Real trends that will provide the real solutions to some pretty massive challenges in the world of health care will come from the world of science, hi-tech and pure research — not from an ongoing, relentless, annoying and ultimately useless amount of hot-air from politicians, regardless of their political stripe.

We need to look at the future of health care from the perspective of medical science, social and demographic trends, the impact of increasing velocity of knowledge and other major trends that have absolutely nothing to do with the political debate around health care reform. You can't wish a problem into a solution — you need pure research and innovation to make things real.

One of the trends that is going to provide tremendous opportunities for innovation in the sector will come about as Silicon Valley sets its sights on health care. Years ago, a senior executive at Intel noted that "*we have the potential to aim our innovation engine at the age wave challenge and change the way we do health care from a crisis- driven, assembly-line, hospital approach to a personal-driven approach, with people taking care of themselves with help from family, friends and technologies.*" At the time they were speaking of health care being one of their top five sources of revenue in the years to come.

One of the biggest growth markets we are beginning to witness now is emerging as Silicon Valley and the hi-tech industry begins to get involved in the world of health care in a whole variety of different ways. First and foremost, it's happening in a very big way with consumer-oriented health care apps, particularly on the iPhone and Android. A recent survey indicated that:

- 78% of consumers are interested in mobile health solutions

- medical and health care apps are the 3rd fast growing category for iPhone and Android phones

- the Apple App store now has 17,000 health care related apps, 60% of which are aimed at the consumer.

We will certainly see a huge amount of product innovation, such as the new iPhone based blood pressure monitor from Withings.

What is really significant is that with such personal medical monitoring and wellness technology, we are going to see very significant involvement by health care providers and professionals, insurers and others within the system to adapt to a new world in which a large number of patients become immersed in the world of interactive healthcare and wellness monitoring.

Then there is the world of bio-connectivity — a trend that will see the emergence of more sophisticated medical device technology that will let medical professionals monitor their patients from afar. Quite simply, in the years to come, the concept of a physical hospital is going to change as it goes virtual through the extension of bio-connectivity technologies and methodologies.

Silicon Valley will also play a huge role as it comes to develop real time health care predictive dashboards and other new forms of medical insight that will help the system to be better predictors of emerging health care risks and crisis situations. Big math, big computers, big analytics and health care – a match made in heaven!

It doesn't stop there. In the world of pharmaceuticals, the impact of Silicon Valley is going to have one of the most dramatic impacts on an industry that we have ever witnessed. For years, the sector has been busy exploring the opportunity for 'pharmacogenetics' — that is, how can we determine if a particular drug treatment is going to have its greatest impact on a group of people who share a common characteristic in their DNA.

This type of very specific genomic medicine has been around for years — but it is about to take off like a rocket as Moore's law comes to have an impact. Quite simply, the cost to do what were once very expensive genetic tests are simply going to plummet.

I could go on as there are dozens of examples where the impact of technology upon the health care system is going to be dramatic. Suffice it to say, if you want to watch one of the trends that will have the most impact in the next decade, this is one of them.

Insurance 2020:
Bold Moves, Turning
Concepts Upside Down!

In an era in which everything around us is plugging together, there are tremendous new opportunities for some pretty massive business model changes in the insurance industry. I often joke that perhaps one day my weigh scale might send an email to my insurance agent letting them know if I'm living up to the terms of my life insurance wellness clause.

Yet, is such thinking far fetched? Maybe not!

One of the biggest trends which is going to hit the world of insurance like a tidal wave is performance based insurance policies. If you live up to or exceed some performance standard, you'll get a rebate or reduction on your insurance policy rate.

It's going to happen extremely quickly in the field of automotive insurance. A flood of GPS enabled performance measuring devices will soon come to inhabit most automobiles throughout the industrialized world. Insurance companies will set a policy price, and then give you a rebate if you exhibit better than average behavior. Consider a program already underway in the UK:

> Insure The Box measures drivers' mileage, when they drive, and how they drive. Excessive G-forces, sudden braking or cornering and long periods of driving without a break are monitored. Policyholders are charged by the mile and motorists initially pay for 6,000 miles. Once these are used up they can buy more miles as they need them. Policyholders are rewarded with "free" miles if they drive safely.
> *Money: A spy in the car that could cut cost of cover for young drivers, The Guardian, UK, April 2011*

You can expect most North American insurance companies to roll out similar technology and performance. Or maybe not — some organizations won't have the speed, agility and flexibility to do this at the pace that the market, competitive and customer pressure will require. The result is a classic opportunity for big business model disruption.

The same type of thing is going to occur in the world of life insurance. It has long been the assumption that despite the rapid emergence of genomic and preventative medicine, that it would never be desirable, ethical or even fair to underwrite policies based on a DNA test.

I'm a believer that this is a pretty big assumption to make. History shows that assumptions that underlie a business model barely last. When I speak about innovation, I advise people it's often best to challenge assumptions — those who don't often miss the biggest opportunities.

Clearly, we know that there are some powerful trends at work:

- the cost for a DNA test that can be used to predict with a high degree of accuracy the diseases and conditions you will inherit in your lifetime is set to collapse, as Moore's law comes to drive down the cost of DNA sequencing machines that do the test

- hence, greater numbers of people will have the opportunity to gain such insight (whether it be good or bad)

- those who have a test that shows a life that will be relatively disease and condition free would likely be able to offer themselves up to a group of speciality insurers and get a policy discount compared to the average population.

Again, there's opportunity for big business model change and upheaval as this happens.

So, too, is the concept of a rebate of your life, medical or disability insurance, if you can prove that you are taking regular, active steps to ensure that you are in good health. Certainly there are those in the health care system who know that with the massive challenges in front of them, a lot of big, bold transformative thinking is necessary.

A federal grant program authorized in the health overhaul law is offering states $100 million to reward Medicaid recipients who make an effort to quit smoking or keep their weight, blood pressure or cholesterol levels in check. The grant program is meant to encourage states to experiment with an uncertain approach to wellness: offering incentives for healthy behavior. *Healthy behaviors pay off; Medicaid recipients who commit to improving their health will be eligible for financial rewards, Los Angeles Times, April 2011*

Extend this type of thinking into what comes next in our hyper-connected world — individuals who monitor their blood pressure, glucose levels and other vitals and are willing to share them with their insurer; exercise and wellness apps on their iPhone that they can use to demonstrate the commitment to a regular series of workouts; adherence to a personalized lifestyle plan — with insurance cost reductions based on performance. This type of stuff isn't far-fetched at all. And it's going to hit the insurance world quicker than it thinks.

Then there's the issue of the underwriting of insurance risk. Today, in the life insurance industry, you must undergo a battery of medical and blood tests so that they can make an assessment if you are insurable or not. Tomorrow will be completely different, and it will be here before the industry knows it:

> Assuming privacy regulations require it, by 2020 underwriting will consist of one question: 'Can I look up everything about you?'
> *The Next Decade in Innovation, Insurance & Technology, May 2011*

Tomorrow? They might simply look you up on Facebook, and based on what they see, come to a decision as to whether they will insure you or not. Farfetched? Not at all! In fact, some in the insurance industry are already talking about it:

> Insurers are preparing to use people's Facebook profiles and online spending habits as a way of setting premiums based on their lifestyle.
> *The Sunday Times, December 2010*

The article goes on to note:

> Studies for the insurers suggest that people's online data detailing their food purchases, activities and social groups can be as good an indicator of their life expectancy as conventional medical examinations. The trials were conducted by Deloitte Consulting LLP and showed that consumer data, based on a sample of 60,000 people, was as effective in identifying potential health risks as if the applicant for insurance had gone for a blood and urine test Aviva, one of Britain's largest insurers, is planning to introduce the new "predictive modelling" in Britain next year after studying the results of trials in America. Swiss Re is also working on a similar scheme.
> *The Sunday Times, December 2010*

The bottom line is that in the next several years, at a very fast pace, the world of insurance is going to be challenged through innovation involving analytics and predictive modeling, performance based policies, and a whole series of other opportunity.

Time For A Little Innovation Oxygen!
Everyone Needs To Inhale Deeply...

Is your organization getting a tad stale? Try rejuvenating staff by prescribing a dose of newfound creativity – through some innovation oxygen!

When my good friend Scott Kress summited Mount Everest, he used a little bit of oxygen for the final push. Many climbers do — sometimes you need the extra energy to accomplish something massive! (Scott's also a speaker, and has a great stage story to tell! When he summited the highest peak in Europe, he ended up in a hi-jacked Russian plane!)

So it is with innovation — sometimes you need some help to accomplish great things. Here are some thoughts on how you can kick up your innovation efforts a bit more. Most importantly, the idea is that you can generate a little innovation oxygen by investing in some experiential capital!

What's the use of innovation oxygen?

It is no secret that we are in an economy that has become far more hurried, complex and uncertain. Things are changing at a furious pace out there – from the products we are selling, to the markets we are selling to, to the attitudes of the customers that we are dealing with. Not to mention challenges with business models, marketing, branding, customer service, new forms of competition — and well, just about everything else!

Faster is the new fast!

In such an environment, a constant, relentless focus on innovative ideas might be the key to helping deal with rapid change. Through innovation, you may discover new opportunities. This is the perfect time for every organization to put in place what I call "innovation oxygen." This involves establishing a culture where everyone is actively encouraged to test a new idea.

In other words, everyone needs to inhale. Oxygen. Innovation oxygen. Breathe it in deeply!

How do you do this? Several ways!

Banish complacency

Start out by banishing forever one of the worst phrases ever to be used in the corporate setting: "We've always done it that way." Let go of the past. Things are different today, and will be far more different tomorrow. Constant, relentless change with markets, products, technology, customer behaviors and attitudes is the new reality.

Trying to go forward by doing what you've done in the past, results in being blind about potential opportunity. Don't let complacency drive your agenda.

Put an alternative culture in place – one that encourages the use of the phrase, "Why not try doing it this way?" If you did things in a certain way in the past and it isn't working as well as it used to then do something completely different. See if it works.

Learn from it if it doesn't work, and move on to something new again. Try ten different approaches, and maybe you'll find one that is effective. Throw out the other 9, and give yourself marks for innovation.

Take risks, reward failure

Of course, you can't do this if your corporate mindset is one that discourages risk-taking. I'd suggest that to get into innovation mode, you should put yourself back in the mindset that existed before the current economic downturn.

Back then, it seemed that almost anything was possible, and everyone was willing to go out on a limb to try something new. That's no longer the case today. The challenges with the economy have had a huge impact on our willingness to try new ways of doing things.

Indeed, it's fair to say that the climate towards risk taking and innovation has become very negative. After all, who would dare to stick out their neck today when they're terrified of losing their job? Everyone is hunkering down, in survival mode.

Such an attitude will certainly help to kill an organization before the recovery even begins!

Bring back the courage to innovate

Otherwise, current attitudes will settle in like a wet sponge, smothering any chance for innovation. Explore new ways of dealing with customers, particularly around social networking. Continue to examine methods of building sustainable customer relationships and loyalty. Return to experimenting with leading edge technology that might help to encourage new methods of building or enhancing brand image.

Whatever the case may be, keep trying out new approaches to do business, and reward those staff members who are willing to experiment and try new ideas.

Deal with the reality of aggressive indecision

Anyone involved in business has come to realize that over the last several years, it has become more and more difficult to close a deal. Massive indecision has come to be the rule, not the exception. You can expect that to be a long-term reality, so adjust your plans accordingly.

The fact is, people have decided not to make decisions – and they like it! This has taught them something – they can hold off on deciding until the very last minute. The impact is rather challenging. It means a business cycle that increasingly relies on long lead times, with sudden and instant short-term decision horizons.

Are you in sales? Here's the new reality — you will find that your prospects will keep putting you off, and then one day will call, breathless and in a rush! There's a decision to be made by tomorrow morning, you are told. They need a revised proposal by 9am, and they need you to attend the meeting. Oh, and you've got to be able to address multiple different product scenarios that haven't been talked about before!

Can you respond to such a situation? Do you have a culture that would let you instantly jump in and reconfigure a deal? Can you pull together the information that would be necessary to support your presentation?

In retrospect, the need to be in an innovative frame of mind becomes obvious – critical, in fact. This new world can present a big shift in the approach that needs to be taken by your team.

Executives must constantly probe and learn how to deal with a business environment in which aggressive indecision is driving the decision making process.

Encourage frivolous education and promote offbeat time

To get into a frame of mind of acting fast, everyone needs to be able to learn a lot, very quickly. One way of doing that is by encouraging people to "waste time." That's right – I really recommend that as a business strategy.

How can people understand the high velocity change in markets, business models, competitive challenges, the emergence of new means of marketing and branding, and all kinds of other issues, if they are restricted to formal education programs? How can they learn about the new products that they need to sell when those products are coming to market so quickly? How can they learn new methods of dealing with a customer by taking an in-house course that was developed over a year ago, when the market was completely different from today?

That's where frivolous education comes in, as a complement to traditional, formal corporate education programs.

Why not establish some "playtime" with your sales force, the purpose of which is to try out a multitude of new technologies: encourage browsing through industry magazines, surfing the Web for market research, etc. Such activities may help bring understanding to how the customer is changing. So in fact, what may appear to be "wasting time," really is not so.

Set your sales force out to do frivolous activities with a goal in mind – to measure customer service, examine competitive activities, take a look at new products, or simply come up with some innovative, new ideas that might help them sell more. Maybe you'll get some unique insight that doesn't come from your traditional educational programs!

Destroy organizational sclerosis

It's been said before, but needs to be said again – hierarchy is the enemy of innovation. Everyone knows that the biggest challenge in many organizations are uncommunicative departments, and a culture that doesn't promote openness. To improve the ability of an organization to innovate, communication barriers need to be broken down.

It seemed that when new technologies appeared on the scene in the 1990's, that there were vast new opportunities to destroy "organizational sclerosis. This culture of open communication is slowly being destroyed, as companies come to discourage frivolous employee communications. Jokes are frowned upon, and political correctness has become stifling.

This indictment of open communication impairs the very ability of the organization to encourage a culture of knowledge exchange, often critical for understanding how markets and customers are changing.

We need to continue to encourage employees to communicate as much as possible, however frivolous. Do this, and you'll find that the culture of innovation opens up too.

Invest in experiential capital

In a world in which business models, methods of customer interaction, and other fundamentals are changing overnight, it's critically important that an organization constantly enhance the skills, capabilities and insight of their people.

They do this by constantly working on projects that might have an uncertain return and payback — but which will provide in-depth experience and insight into change.

It's by understanding change that opportunity is defined, and that's what experiential capital happens to be. In the future, it is one of the most important assets that you can possess.

*   *   *   *   *

ABOUT THE AUTHOR

Jim Carroll is one of the world's leading international futurists, trends and innovation experts, with a client list that ranges from Northrop Grumman to Johnson & Johnson, the Swiss Innovation Forum to the National Bank of Australia, the Walt Disney Organization to NASA. His focus is on helping to transform growth oriented organizations into high velocity innovation heros.

An author, columnist, media commentator and consultant, he has spent the last two decades providing direct, independent guidance to a huge, diverse client base. He has provided his insight for countless industry sectiors including life sciences, health care, insurance, manufacturing, agriculture, technology, government, retail, banking, to name but a few.

One of his recent events was for the PGA - the Professional Golf Association of America. Jim loves to golf, but isn't very good at it, which caused him some amazement when he was invited to open their 94th Annual General Meeting. Jim was the first outside speaker the PGA had ever engaged to speak at their AGM. During his session he challenged the 500 golf pros in attendance to think about innovation and future trends. Jim has high hopes that he has helped to shape the future direction of the world's largest sport.

He's also hoping to inspire you in a similar way through the content in this book.

Jim and his wife and business partner, Christa, have worked together out of a home office in Mississauga, Ontario for over 20 years. Their sons, Willie and Tom, have come to understand that a great partnership comes from a combination of the different skills that each parent brings to a project such as this book, ranging from creativity to editorial insight, deep thinking to complex project management.

Invest in experiential capital, and that's where you'll find your innovation oxygen.